Nocturnal Whispers

Peter,
I hope you enjoy my
works and hope to
see you again soon!

Michael Angelo
Lipps

6-17-2017
St Louis
Gateway
Con

Books by Michael Angelo Sippo

Drifting Seasons
Nocturnal Whispers
Archangels: The Eden Conspiracy*

*Coming Soon

Nocturnal Whispers

Michael Angelo Sippo

authorHOUSE®

AuthorHouse™ LLC
1663 Liberty Drive
Bloomington, IN 47403
www.authorhouse.com
Phone: 1-800-839-8640

Published by AuthorHouse   08/28/2013

ISBN: 978-1-4918-1321-8 (sc)
ISBN: 978-1-4918-1320-1 (e)

Library of Congress Control Number: 2013915400

Table of Contents

For all those up at night worried and praying for a better tomorrow, that this helps you rest with sweet dreams and instills hope as you awake to a bright new morning.

Acknowledgements

I would like to especially thank Christine who helped with editing and has supported all my work. Thank you for all your feedback and for being a wonderful friend!

I would like to thank my family for their support, especially my mother Isa and sister Isabel who helped with editing and organizing the book. Thank you for all your encouragement and never ending support!

In Memory

of

Sean M. Sippo

. . . Sleep Tight . . .

Sweet Dreams

The night is calling for you to rest
Cuddled in the hold of the mattress' chest
May all your worries become a mere jest
And under celestial twinkles may you be blessed

I wish for you only dreams so sweet
Sailing the seas of clouds in a flying fleet
Or embracing someone special whom you've been waiting to meet
May all your fantasies be a magical treat

Whether soothed by a warm sunset ray
Refreshed in cool waters of a tranquil bay
Or sitting in a field of flowers fresh in May
That all provide you a smile for the next day

To roam the skies as free as a dove
To finally be with the one you love
Let your head rest in the feathery glove
While being watched over tenderly from above

May a world of pure imagination you meet
Let its serenity and peace sweep you off your feet
Explore your own universe wondrous and neat
May you have dreams that are so sweet

The Edge (Outcasts Unite)

Well I'm an outlaw
A wanted misfit of night
The rebel in the brawl
A creature out of sight

The creepy shadow instilling fear
That brings even an erotic thrill
The hunter drawing near
Closing in for the kill

Live on the edge
Outcasts unite
Live on the edge
Outcasts unite

Calling all outcasts it's time to unite
Take it all straight to the fight
Live on the edge just to survive
Anything goes just to stay alive

Calling all exiles, join the deprived
Show the world how we have strived
Live on the edge with no fear in sight
This is our time, outcasts unite

Yeah I'm a mongrel
The leader of alley scum
The phantom of control
There's nothing I can't overcome

Into the streets I come out to play
The top dog you better evade
In my yard we do things my way
Destroying all who dare to invade

Calling all outcasts it's time to unite
Take it all straight to the fight
Live on the edge just to survive
Anything goes just to stay alive

Calling all exiles, join the deprived
Show the world how we have strived
Live on the edge with no fear in sight
This is our time, outcasts unite

Mask

And I'd give everything up for you
To show the real man that lies behind
Yet could you bear what is true
Can you love the person you'll find

But it could deepen the wound I cannot heal
So I wait until you are out of sight
Only then my identity I will reveal
Staring alone at my mask at night

With it all the pain and suffering hide
Covering sorrow of a heart broken
Concealing the tears I bleed inside
Silencing the words I want spoken

I wonder how the world would see me
Do they only prefer me with my mask
When can I live without the mystery
To accept me for who I am is all I ask

Silence fills the dense air
A kingdom dormant with despair
Choked by a forest of dead blades
That holds a gentle maid

Cursed with a dire fate
By a prick of greed and hate
That would end her days of tomorrow
Leaving all in the castle with sorrow

Yet one fairy's wish freezes all time
So none would live with this crime
Sparing all a painful weep
Just putting them in an erosionless sleep

A princess once left for dead
Now rests her sweet head
Waiting for her prince instead

In slumber floating in the heaven's sea
In a tower above every thorny tree
Dreams the sleeping beauty

To awake in the morning light
With her true love in sight
From one kiss all would be set right

To arise from the sleeping sands
And together revive the lands
Just by taking each other's hands

In the distance, set on a destined course
A young prince travels by horse
On a journey he can't comprehend
Searching over the horizon's bend

A future he had been assigned
Yet all this he leaves behind
Evading his father's choice
Only to follow a mysterious voice

From his dreams an angel calls
Lying inside these castle walls
Wrapped in vines of twisted thorns
There a rose waits to be born

A princess once left for dead
Now rests her sweet head
Waiting for her prince instead

In slumber floating in the heaven's sea
In the tower above every thorny tree
Dreams the sleeping beauty

To awake in the morning light
With her true love in sight
From one kiss all would be set right

To arise from the sleeping sands
And together revive the lands
Just by taking each other's hands

At the bridge's gates the prince arrives
Yet he's stopped in his drive
For the evil witch did appear
Sensing her spell's end was near

As more thorns filled the lawn
Into a dark dragon she did spawn
Risking everything in her last stand
To crush true love with her own hand

Yet the prince would not yield
Instead he readies his righteous shield
Drawing his sword of virtue to attack
For nothing will hold him back

Victorious from the fierce clash
With the dragon left in ash
The spiked vines untwine
As the prince runs up the tower's spine

With the passing of each flight
The sky fills more with the dawn's light
All the cumbersome fog starts to disappear
As to the top the prince draws near

And entering through the door
He finds the lady that he adores
Captivated by her tender glow
He leans towards her slow

And down on one knee
Letting their lips touch gently
He kisses the sleeping beauty

Oh Aurora, awake in the morning light
With your true love in sight
For his kiss has set all right

Arise from the sleeping sands
And together revive the lands
While embraced in each other's hands

Let all the kingdom see
A true love that is meant to be
The prince and his beauty

I stand out from the rest of my kind
For I'm the only one with no partner to find
I'm the seed from which roots and branches begin
Yet if you backtrack, you'll notice I'm the last of kin

I am the symbol of what many dread
Except when linked and stretched on the trail of black
Unless they were drowning in a sea of red
Then I'm the lifesaver who brought them back

I always remain on the neutral side
For into factions I will not divide
You may add me to your group at no extra cost
And cut me when you like with no expenses lost

But those who cross me have no chance
For all fail to have me break and fracture
And my abilities none can amplify or enhance
For I always remain in the same stature

But do not confuse me to be a god
Or to fall under the category as being odd
And though I was the last character to enlist
In reality, I do not even exist

Made Man

Whether jackin' a Mustang from the street
Or scouring the alleys for a hooker to meet
Locked in my crib with just powder to snort
It just another day escaping my date in court

Just jaunting in the district looking for fun
While keeping the trigger ready on my gun
Some may ask why did I turn to a life of crime
What they don't understand is this is my prime

I'm a made man, not some steady jobber
I whack whoever the Don wants me to clobber
I am on the top and there is nothing to lose
So I thought, till it came to which family to choose

Yeah a few nights I was rabid and wild
Ended up marrying to support a child
Yet no longer was I able to manage the wife
So I ditched them only for a mob life

And with that our vows were torn apart
And she moved elsewhere with him for a new start
But why did I even try and bother
I turned out worse than my father

So feeling down I went to a local bar
There I was praised as the rising star
My suit pockets were all stuffed with cash
I'm popular with the girls and got my own stash

My work shown in the obituaries to be read
Thanks to me, yeah that punk is dead
Yet I wonder when I'll be ash in an urn
And my name appears on the next paper's turn

But all my worries now are smoked out by drugs
For I gave up on receiving my son's hugs
Still often I turn to my mother
Telling her that this new kid is like my brother

At the pole dance, boy did he whistle and shout
But I hope this time I won't have to take this one out
Another one thinking he will be the next made man
Try all you want, but honestly I don't think he can

He's a nice kid, though he's too abrupt
He switches sides and is easily corrupt
For all we know he could be a cop's rat
And it is my job to make sure we have none of that

But I wonder could the good Lord forgive each attack
Would he be willing to take this sinner back
Oh later I think I can quickly pray
Only asking though to get through another day

Just to buy more time by dodging another cop
Yet sometimes wondering when will it stop
For now I just let it drown in my drink
Still pondering if I will swim or sink

But hey I don't mean to gloat
My head's above water, I'm still afloat
You cross me wrong, I'll fill you with lead
Mess on my turf, you'll end up like the others . . . dead

My mission is to protect the human race
Yet sometimes I feel it is my kind taking its place

My skin now an internal organ under steel
Prodded with copper nerves with an artificial feel

A shot of confidential steroids tightens the reflexes for speed
More drugs and serums replace the blood I used to bleed

My brain now is even technologically enhanced
Allowing all senses to detect enemies miles in their advance

Trained to lose the emotions all humans hold
The heart only left to beat blood running cold

The new super soldier in iron clad
The military's newest hardware . . . and current fad

Yet my successful transformation was to many a surprise
For in the transfusion, two thirds of the squad met their demise

Wondering if they'll be sent to the strip yard instead of the morgue
Where parts can be recycled from a failed or old modeled cyborg

But there is no time or reason to show remorse
My new deployment and mission are already on course

My identity has been completely redone
Just a soldier numbered Delta-Zero-One

Force to breathe the cloaking poison mist
While snow blinded by the detonated smoke
Led by the snout guided by my wrist
While its Adam's apple I'm ready to choke

Wandering into the eye of the stormy weather
Where ash and shrapnel sleet and rain
All being preyed under a keen black feather
As the mother land cries in fright and pain

The inferno stained horizon snarls and roars
As a city is digested in the abyss' stomach growl
While plumes of fire hiss and soar
Forcing people to scatter like desperate fowl

The oncoming herd makes the blood boil hotter
As tension in the muscles tries to take the controls
But there's no reason to go into the savage slaughter
Death has already had its fill of the innocent souls

The flesh and brew splattered in endless labyrinth blocks
As the atmosphere is fogged in a stench of rotting musk
Bones clattering while the ground nervously rocks
All ripped and chewed by another piercing tusk

Still chaos waves in the tremoring crowd
While in the vicinity stalks a hungry pack
Using fallen rubble as their shroud
Waiting for an opportune moment to attack

Chameleons embracing the settling dust
Assuming the appearance of a chick and hen
Yet no stirring my guard can trust
For it could be a wolf hiding in the pen

Am I seen as the lantern shining hope's light
Will they accept the trust of an unknown soldier
Or do they peer in monster eyes red in sight
Perceiving a merciless assassin growing colder

Yet all it takes is one pup's scream
Now the swarm is alert and alive
For in the air molten stingers now beam
Empting a nest of a buzzing hive

Another deadly egg about to hatch
My position now they try to hone
And the hungry vultures rapidly dispatch
Encircling around my sanctuary zone

Yet they are nothing but poor helpless fools
Drawn by the broken armor in which I'm clad
Not realizing I'm the game master making the rules
They are the prey who now have it coming bad

How for a breath I could show them pity
Let them wander this day out of lament
Yet when they choose to welcome me with that committee
All I can think now is that they will be forced to repent

For we roam in a jungle of war
Where odds are obscured and never fair
With death always knocking behind the door
The only survivors are the ones who dare

And now my prey's advance I prepare to stunt
Falling into my trap readied by keen sense
I'm the predator waiting now to finish the hunt
One short burst, then all will echo silence

The numbers keep piling as they try
It matters not if I'm seen a villain or hero
For my kind never do die
And all eventually return to zero

I had a dream that a soldier cried
As I laid in his arms and slowly died
He leaned towards me to offer a kiss
Yet my late lips gave him only emptiness

From his heart shined a light of gold
And a ring trickled down from an opened fold
By my paling hand it landed near
Yet on my finger another band did leer

Then silence was killed by a clicking gun
Aimed by a shadow standing before the sun
At the soldier it unleashed the fiery lead
As the trigger finger linked me to the man I wed

I was ripped from the darkness of the dream
But was too out of breath to release my scream
As reality settled around me alone and cold
Leaving me to shiver in my own comforting hold

Staring at the nightstand by my bed's side
Glancing at my love a still frame eyed
Then at a letter written and another read
While the memories skipped inside my head

Where I am standing across another friend
One who would keep my secrets till the very end
We would never be too far away
We would always be near we both would say

Then one day came the breaking news
His company for awhile I would have to lose
For the world now blistered in a bloody battle
And he was herded as one of the army's cattle

The day I saw him go off to war
He told me there was no lady for him to adore
He asked if I could be his soldier's sweetheart
So with our letters we wouldn't seem so far apart

I smiled at him as I agreed
To hear of his safety I would dearly need
I reached out to embrace him in a hug
And for a second he jerked back like by a tug

But into my arms he gently stuttered
And under his breath three sounds he muttered
What they were I did not know
I just held him tight hoping he wouldn't go

Yet I stood and watched as our eyes teared
And then in the crowd he just disappeared
I felt each moment of time go by
Waiting until his plane was swallowed in the sky

Four weeks had been frozen still
Every day I grew more pale and ill
Then finally one evening I received a letter
And seeing his writing made me feel better

How every word grew my smile
Each sentence seemed to stretch a mile
Oh how I laughed when he ended with "Love"
And with X's and O's lined up above

And since being his wartime sweetheart
I made sure to keep up with my part
Sometimes writing back with added perfume
Hoping to make him blush while others fume

Even when someone else I started to court
The sweetheart antics we didn't abort
Still sending stories and thoughts to share
Writing as if sitting with each other there

Yet recent events have my life confused
The last several nights this dream has abused
All coming after the last letter I had composed
Telling him how the one I see plans to propose

While there was excitement in the words I drew
An uneasiness in my chest slowly grew
And it was after my name had been signed
That the dismay had finally poured into my mind

It was a friendly joke for me at the start
Spraying a cheap fragrance and spelling love with a heart
Yet soon I became indecisive on choosing a brand
And ensuing words were more caressed by my hand

18

It was after writing "P.S.—I love you so much"
That the feeling was amplified by a tearful touch
Then about the day we parted I began to ponder
And I realized then he was looking for something fonder

Now I wish that I could find a way
To go back and correct that yesterday
For I see his hug was meant to be a kiss
And I want to hear those words my ear did miss

So now I wait to again see his face
To feel his warmth as we tenderly lace
And before giving him the kiss that's due
To hear him say those three words . . . "I love you"

There were things I never wanted you to know
Yet I am here with defenses down
To you now I am willing to show
Able to reveal what this costume does gown

I may appear to be ruthless and vicious
Yet the blood in my veins doesn't run that cold
Though my character at times seems suspicious
It's just a persona that my mask does hold

So I ask, take a good look at my face
See the real me that it used to replace
This but a symbol that everyone can pride
But you . . . you deserve to see what lies inside

I know sometimes I don't make sense
At times I'm insecure, having little confidence
Fearing my faults and weaknesses you would see
Witnessing just how screwed up I could be

How I'm still shrouded in my past
Where all the pain and anger forever last
Feeding my inner ambitions for revenge
And creating this image to avenge

Wanting to ensure no one would suffer a dire fate
Yet so much already the commitment ate
For while protecting others from all crime
My alter ego took up the majority of my own time

I had such a need to protect
That my own future I had to neglect
Relationships and dreams would have to wait
But I didn't realize it would be this late

Always concerned first with the mission
Preventing me from pursuing another ambition
So in my mask I would travel far
While my real identity became the shadow's scar

Yet you were the one to make it bleed
And a once forgotten person you freed
And so much more came into view
All this I realized because of you

My perspective does not need to focus on the one oath
For if I work hard, I can actually achieve both
In others' lives I can still become a part
While I hold those dear to me in my heart

I now know there is more in life to share
And as I experience it, I want you to be there
For you have become the motivation in my drive
You are the reason I want to be alive

I know this may be too much to understand
Yet I hope through it all, you'll be holding my hand
I promise to you nothing more I will hide
All I ask is that you remain by my side

So here I am, completely unmasked
Showing you the truth, just like you asked
What do you think of my true identity
Will you accept the person that is really me

Treasured Smile

I do not know where to start
All the words I cannot find
To thank you from the bottom of my heart
And honor a person so lovely and kind

From lying together along the roaring beach
From wishing upon the nights shooting stars
Or helping me translate your native speech
Or weaving around pot holes together by car

From being teased by your uncle's jokes
Or told by all "coma más comida"
While traveling to craters and cones pluming smoke
Or visiting tu familia en la finca

From the canopy trees which we'd swing
To all the markets where we could shop
While traveling through the lands of eternal spring
Or even navigating through a cloudy mountain top

With every friend and family I was able to meet
With every dance and karaoke sung
Everything was so memorable and sweet
And all the time spent with you was fun

Yet I will always have this fondest memory
For this alone made my trip worthwhile
Just when you turned looking at me so lovely
And giving me your joyful smile

Whether saying good morning in the early dawns
Or as you passed by while making the house clean
Or as you brushed your teeth and put make-up on
Your gentle smile made all a pleasurable scene

And I know this is not the last goodbye
For we will have more time together to share
Yet if you happen to witness me as I cry
Know that each tear shows how much for you I care

With every word that we say
With any activity that we do
You always bring happiness in my day
And I enjoy every second with you

And by talking together on the phone
With all our pictures that I see
Even just by reading your emails alone
I feel you are right there beside me

Ever since we met from the start
You have been a wonderful and special friend
And you will always have a place in my heart
With love that will never end

And know that you will always be on my mind
That you will always be in my prayers
And that I will be waiting for the day I turn to find
You smiling at me and standing there

My Australian Rose

I met her when she was sweet sixteen
She lived in Tassy is what I was told
Though distance and barriers lay in-between
A special friendship began to unfold

During the quiet nights she opened her mind
Her thoughts and stories she did share
A gentle soul so sweet and kind
More and more for her I grew in care

So strange it does seem
To get so close with one far apart
Yet like a heavenly angel from a dream
She quickly won this American bloke's heart

However our messages broken by a silent tide
Unknowingly one day, we left each other's side

Alone I laid myself in bed
Wondering during the restless night
Was it something that I could have said
While hoping her days were going alright

I continued with the studies' strife
New friends and activities I did find
Yet while staying at pace with the rapid life
I still could never get her out of my mind

Then one night, a familiar icon I did see
So back on the chat I did sign
Suddenly my heart skipped and pondered "Could it be"
For there was my long, lost Caroline

With a simple line of characters, the silence finally did end
Reunited at last, I caught up with my Australian friend

Though she begins her busy work day
As I come home from mine at night
We always have plenty to say
And every letter from her is such a delight

One evening we told of our sad ordeal
How at times we felt so alone
Yet taking the step we thought was unreal
The first time we heard each other on the phone

That one call brought laughter and a smile
Leading her to calling me twice
Even though we chatted only a little while
A simple goodbye could not suffice

For you asked of me the dreams down the line
Now I will share with you a special one of mine

Willing to endure a tedious flight
Just to see your pretty and loving face
Longing for the joyous sight
To welcome you with a warm embrace

To finally be able to hold you near
To feel your soft golden hair
Allowing me to wipe your tear
And whisper to you how much I care

From you no feelings I can hide
Looking in your eyes sparkling bright
For when you are by my side
Everything just seems so right

To you I say this openly and true
My dear, with all my heart . . . I love you

Yo-Yo

You really know how to pull my string
Always getting me to wrap around your finger
Giving me a tight rope to desperately cling
Or leaving me in my cradle to rock and linger

Once in a while you take me on a walk
Sometimes we get to travel around the world
Yet you also place me in a convenient lock
Or out of interest I am rudely hurled

At times you let the attachment sag and slack
Other instances just leave my head spinning
Then at an opportune moment you yank me back
Expecting to start again from the beginning

But I am glad that I can bring you some joy
Even if I am still only perceived as just a toy

Sometimes I wonder what's on your mind
For why do you keep this so blind
It has many varieties, so pick one kind
Surely it couldn't be that hard to find

It may have worked in your history
But don't rely on just a mere reflection
For without it, you can leave one in eternal mystery
And also suffering from the greatest rejection

Fail to use it, and yourself you will isolate
Or make someone a little annoyed or irate
Even having others to worry and wait
Then you find it when it's now too late

And using it doesn't take much time
To think that you ought to receive a scold
For I even implement it in this rhyme
It is so easy, do not be so cold

In the morning on the porch we sat down
She was dressed in her pink evening gown
How I have adored her from far away
Thinking of the right words to say
To drive out any thoughts that'd make her frown

And I saw her shivering as the winds blew colder
So I reached out my arms just to hold her
To warm her in my embrace
And rest her pretty face
To lay her head on my open shoulder

Together we sat for awhile
At every glance I'd see her smile
She was so glad to be with me
That her eyes had shown me
And I realized now her tender care
That no words were needed to share
For I'm just happy she is there

In the morning light I sat by his side
My voice remained shy and seemed to hide
I hadn't known him for long
Yet my feelings for him had grown strong
When in my presence alone he did reside

And with his gentle smile that I'd receive
All the worries and fears began to leave
With my fingers in his palm
His touch made me calm
And I rested in every breath that he'd breathe

Together we sat for awhile
At every glance I'd see him smile
He was glad to be with me
That his eyes had shown me
And I realize now his tender care
That no words were needed to share
For I'm just happy he is there

Together we sit for awhile
At every glance I see you smile
You are so glad to be with me
That your eyes now show me
And I realize now your tender care
No words are needed for us to share
For I'm just happy that you are there

There are feelings that are hard to find
Usually confusing to the mind
Yet seem to be so true
As I stand here thinking of you

Leaves you anxious with nothing to say
But embraces emotions in a different way
Just longing to hear your name
Tell me do you feel the same

Where time is not what it seems
Is this reality or another dream
Just a fantasy unseen
What does is all mean

And then I see our destiny in your loving eyes
And I hear our future sing in your lullabies
I can feel each moment as you take my hand
The answers found now I understand
This love can't hold us apart
And it's calling each other's heart

There are questions that the mind still hold
Leaving you feeling all empty and cold
With worries you don't want to say
Will mystery and pain drive us away

What if this is not what we perceived
Just another stranger to be received
Leaving me without you
What am I supposed to do

But when I see and touch your pretty face
It tells me we've found our rightful place
As our fingers interweave
Asking each other not to leave

And then I see our destiny in your loving eyes
And I hear our future sing in your lullabies
I can feel each moment as you take my hand
The answers found now I understand
This love can't hold us apart
And it's calling each other's heart

Let's lay all our fears to rest
Together facing life's long test
Every step for us to define
With our smiles that brightly shine

This night we finally stand all alone
This special moment making our own
Letting our emotions freely sing
And telling each other the joys we bring

Time stands still just for you and me
To share our feelings the way it's meant to be
Kissing softly and hugging tight
While dancing under the star light

We can take our hands and run down the street
Laughing together as I sweep you off your feet
Writing our true love song
And cuddlin' close at the light of dawn

And then I see our destiny in your loving eyes
And I hear our future sing in your lullabies
I can feel each moment as you take my hand
The answers found now I understand
This love can't hold us apart
And it's calling each other's heart

Trying to open up to a fellow member
Yet they badger back and do not understand
With this one, it has been too long to remember
The other will receive late the messages by hand

I give a friend a call, yet receive no sound
Another one is out, but I don't know where
I knock on a neighbor's door, yet no one to be found
Just searching for someone who could be there

Instead left with my thoughts, sitting all alone
Wondering where are those whom I've given so much time
Laying on the couch, waiting by the phone
Feeling like I am a victim of a crime

For many I tossed my duties and worries aside
To give my full attention to their issues that burn
To help at any hour and in anyway I always tried
Yet I never see the same when it is my turn

So seconds bleed as tears are cried
Which only God is willing to see
As silently I beg that the answers no longer hide
For I know He holds the path that is best for me

Yes, I know many blessing I have and still receive
That I do recognize and can never ignore or ban
And in His will I do thoroughly believe
Yet do you forget that I am still human

Yes, we are supposed to live in His reflection
But nature gives us emotions to share
And is it not right to ask a question
To pour out my feelings, would you even care

For I dream of having a steady romance
To have my own family to love and kiss
Yet I worry that somehow I'll blow that chance
Or that the opportunity I already did miss

I witness others' lives move actively along
Seeing some having children or finding their mate
To feel a little jealous, is that really so wrong
For it is like forever that I will patiently wait

With my chances, all the best efforts I try to make
Yet still I feel that I always end in last place
Just to look at myself and stare at every mistake
And wonder who would want this sorry face

Oh how I'm told by many that I am special
How they wish they be with someone like me
Yet am I really perceived as being essential
Or is there something that I cannot see

All this my heart and mind continue to bark
As I wade through the long, barren night
Slowly being swallowed by the thick, cold dark
Praying all will be better in the morning light

And I apologize, for I know I seem rude
I do not mean to put any blame on you
I'm just lost and confused in feelings deeply brewed
I feel so abandoned, and don't know what to do

Thief

Who is this crafty thief
That brings one happiness or grief
Always running to steal life
Creeping up to cause strife

Forcing many to nervously wait
While determining the roles of fate
Though some want to see him more
For others he provides an extra chore

Many witness as he comes and goes
Yet often he passes when nobody knows
The mysterious evader eluding the night
While being quicker than the sun's rays of light

In no boundary he is confined
Never being able to fall behind
His tales all historians reflect
While his adventures the oracles always project

Living in memories ancient to the heart
Existing in dreams before they start
Yet for him this very instance does not matter
For any moment he can easily shatter

Said to be the greatest artist unable to be caught
Well . . . I quickly purge that very thought
Though he is as swift as a rocket
From him I can also pickpocket

Defying briefly his intentions by making a stand
Stealing precious grains by my own hand
Not having to be dictated by his design
For I am able to take what is mine

And though I often lose to his heated race
Once in a while he stops and stares in my face
The thief becomes silent and dumb
Letting his precision fingers become numb

And from me nothing he would lift
Offering instead a small, generous gift
And just passing on by calm and kindly
Whispering to me "Use the present wisely"

Thoughts of someone cause you to hesitate
Stress from the job acts as a road block
Finances clog the lungs that ventilate
Overwhelmed nerves put the brain in a deadlock

Worries of the past haunt your dreams
Fears of the future scream in your head
Everything enters wild madness it seems
Leaving you tossing and turning nervously in bed

Running lost in what ifs, drowning in sweat cold
Till suddenly interrupted by a speedy vehicle's zoom
Then slowly falling to the floor as silence takes hold
As heavy breathing fills the emptiness in the room

Yet use this moment when you are alone
Shut your eyes, let the mind clear
Relax the muscles that are gripping each bone
And turn your senses to what is near

Start off by saying a small prayer
Slowly let your voice count to ten
Then lose track of when, forget about where
Just explore the simplicity of Zen

Listen to every tick of the clock
Hear the rhythm of your own heart
Synchronize the beat with every tock
Spread each breath a little further apart

Feel the breath of every follicle and hair
The stream of blood that warms your face
Let the soul sit steady on a pocket of air
While in complete control you are encased

A time of cleansing has calmly begun
Rest peacefully in the nurturing womb
Where the spirit and body again become one
And returning innocence prepares to bloom

Awaken now from what you meditate
Be reborn by opening your eyes
See how the day is far from late
And in nothing, much more now you will realize

Ignite

Out of ashes, into light
Risen in flames that ignite
Wings that span, burning bright
A guardian will awaken this very night

To raise the fallen, to restore the age
Able to unleash an inferno's rage
While all seek to be its cage
It can only belong to one mage

Again the riddles begin to play in my head
Haunting me even before I sleep in death's bed
Knowing now those words were not about me
Only pondering who could my successor be
But in the next repeated verse, I started to see

Residing in one of the family name
In the last child so infant and tame
Now the guardian is hers to claim
And she will be nurtured by its holy flame

But before it ends, previous reflections begin to show
Stay with me, for it'll reveal all you need to know
For in death's gorge I will soon be cast
My time here is short, but I want my story to last
So relive with me my mysterious past

I am among those living in the incantation ages
With lands full of wizards, witches, sorcerers and mages
Where all generations are born under a guardian's sign
Whose mystical soul with the family's head combine
And continues to flow down the successor's bloodline

Whether it be kin, cousin, aunt, or brother
A great uncle or even a step mother
Any member far or near can be the next heir
Usually it resides with the one with the grayest hair
Sometimes it with two, though that legendarily rare

And they do not always reside in the same house
For they can be passed to a married spouse
Or if the last heir's life was to defuse
Then all submissive chains the guardian will lose
And its next master it must freely choose

So several could be passed to a daughter or son
Yet there is another way to get more than one
For if the last drop of blood were to spill
The guardian will fall to the one who'd kill
And be forced to do the murder's will

Thus for power some chose to strive
But many vowed to work together to survive
Pacts were formed and tribes did band
Borders were drawn and villages settled the land
The dawn of civilization was finally at hand

Eventually under one kingdom all would unite
Under the guidance of a couple with great foresight
Creating academies where mages could assist
Building guilds for defenders to enlist
Making it able for all to peacefully coexist

Such leadership and dedication no one had ever seen
And thus the two were made the king and queen
In the highest mountains the monarch today dwells
Residing in the largest academy and library of spells
Hidden in natural barriers and protected by magical shells

All these precautions still needed to be set
For the world was burdened by an evil threat
By the warlocks under Deadlock's rule
A powerful heretic both vile and cruel
Through dark arts he brought suffering and gruel

Using his necromancy to summon the undead
Across the continents their wrath and fury he led
And with the death of each magus soul
More power grew under his control
For bloodlines ended, and guardians he stole

Thus it was an era of battles between eternal life and sleeping death
And being the guild's lead mage of light, all depended on my breath
Yet if I were to fall, none at my funeral would have grieved
For selfish praise my manners and character conceived
However, my guardian was always well received

It could revive all who'd fallen to a slash
Its cleansing flames burned wounds to ash
Restoring strength with its purifying light
Allowing our armies to continue the fight
And it's entrusted in my blood, it's my given right

The Phoenix born of holy fire
Its healing powers all did desire
With it, the favors in battle to us turn
For in its blaze, the enemies easily burn
While our allies continued to live and learn

And I didn't care if I was called a brute
Those who witnessed my magic were left mute
Not only in me does the Phoenix dwell
For I am able to call upon long forgotten spells
And with one cast, legions of enemies usually fell

I was a man of great pride
And that I made sure not to hide
For great power demands great respect
And I was the most needed and useful in every aspect
I had no weaknesses . . . except the family that I would neglect

A loving wife, so tender and mild
Just giving birth to our first child
How I had ambitions of a son so strong
Someone who could honor and carry our name on
Yet I got a daughter, so for now that dream is gone

Sickened as my wife cared for that disgrace
Stuffing her breast in that wretch's face
Deciding that Talon would be her name
To honor the Phoenix, yet I thought it was to shame
She's nothing special; a future kitchen maid and useless dame

But I guess I still owe my wife a bit of thanks
With her connections to the queen, I rose quickly in ranks
Yet it was my own abilities that I used
Taking on dangers even the royal elites refused
Always returning, leaving enemies and allies confused

So for now, they would be my last worry
For I had to race to a town in a hurry
That was under a sudden pincer attack
And we needed to hold the assault back
For the Oracle guardian resided in some shack

Yet we saw the horizon wave in a heated haze
The entire village had already been set ablaze
Already too late to halt the legion's campaign
All we could do was see if anything could remain
So a mage summoned Leviathan to end the fires with rain

Nothing was there but ash and smoke
But it was hard to see under the night's cloak
I searched through the tragedy hidden by a new moon
As angrily I vowed to catch Deadlock soon
While lighting the landscape in my flamed cocoon

With that, I heard a whimpering sound
And noticed something rustling on the ground
A little girl tugging and yanking at her foot
Caught under some rubble, buried like a root
With her eyes closed, temporarily blinded by soot

So I ran towards her yelling that I was drawing near
But the heated glow of my protector's fire brought her fear
And a guardian was summoned from her desperate scream
And towards me it unleashed a blinding white beam
And all I remember was standing alone as if in a dream

There I was surrounded by the dark
And the Phoenix's flame I couldn't spark
Then a figure was carved out of a flare
The Oracle appeared with a piercing stare
Citing a rhyme that chilled the air

> Out of ashes, into light
> Residing with her on this night
> Within her spirit, it will take flight
> In her heart will its fires ignite

> Residing with the last of your name
> Only in a child so innocent and tame
> Yet one would slay her with no shame
> For with that, the guardian he can claim

He spoke in a language that I never heard
Yet somehow I understood his every word
But before I could ask, the guardian disappeared
While two young girls before me appeared
And right at me both nervously peered

One sprouting long, dark cedar locks
Which behind her back the wind rocks
Dressed in the robes of an apprentice mage
Looking to be nearing twenty years of age
Yet too young to have a daughter of this stage

For the little one had seen already a decade
Just below the chin her reddish gold twirls swayed
Wrapped in an ivory tunic, yet covered in ash
And down her right arm blood ran from a punctured gash
As she trembled pale while clutching the mage's sash

Who has done this to her arm
Who is it that wishes you harm
He will have to deal with me now instead
Direct me to where this villain has fled
I will make him pay for every drop you bled

We will not fall for your lies
You are the one that causes alarm
For you have his same look in your eyes
You would lead us to our demise
Why do you wish to bring us harm

My dear, I am a mage of the just
I'm here to help, my words you can trust
Her wound I can help mend and lace
Here, let's wash her pretty face
Let me take you both to a safer place

As I neared them, the child began to cry
And then a young man fell between us from the sky
Having rustic dust running in his eyes and hairs
Strange metal plates instead of robes he wears
And on his left shoulder, a bleeding cut he too bears

Then pulling out a strange staff, silver and thin
Keeping it erect, not letting the point near his shin
Then towards me it fiercely swung
Setting a trail of fire on the run
For right at me, the Phoenix he flung

Shot out of a dream and into a fold
I finally awoken from the suffocating hold
Panting senselessly as my lungs the oxygen fill
Bumps teasing nerves with sweat's trickling chill
As everything slowly halted to a clear standstill

Then I was surrounded by the examining mob
Twirling in questions asked while others sob
Looking around yet seeing a blurry cloud
Till I heard my name called out loud
And saw my wife bursting through the crowd

Oh thank the guardians you are alive
I thought only a corpse there could lay
For you have been cold for over a day
Yet all hope came from what Mira had to say
For the Oracle told her your sense would arrive

Mi . . . ra . . . I know no one of that name
Is she the next one the Oracle had to claim
What happened to me the other night
All I recall was a blinding light
Followed by a dream of pure fright

Wait, we must now hurry back
I must revive those fallen to the attack
Someone, fetch my staff and gown
Argh . . . why do I have such pain on my crown
And why do you all just stand and frown

Mira was the only one that survived
She was the little girl that you found
All the rest remain buried in the ground
And since the sun has already traveled around
The hour has passed for them to be revived

And she had you attacked, but it was a mistake
She felt your fire and thought it was a second raid
And unconsciously she called the Oracle for aid
Giving you cuts and wounds that have yet to fade
But she's sorry, and was waiting with me for you to awake

Feeling the western hemisphere of my globe
There a fissure my fingers began to probe
The crevasse opened wide and deep
Out of wells pus and blood still seep
And a gentle brush set pain running steep

And as I saw her standing worried there
I realized she was the same girl from my nightmare
Because of her I had these wounds to find
And then she has her guardian pollute my mind
All this caused my muscles to tensely wind

How I considered her a worthless brat
And at her guardian Oracle I would spat
For they gave me a near fatal incision
And cursed me with a strange vision
That my mind continues to show without my decision

Running down my chest stretched too a fresh scar
And seeing that the little culprit wasn't too far
I stormed to her as I raised my trembling hand
Yet I was stopped, for between us my wife and child stand
Holding firm, not even budging at my fierce command

Get out of the way of that witch
Don't you see the gape I can't stitch
I tried to help her and with this I'm repaid
Well an example here will now be made
With the rest of the rubble she should have stayed

Would you dare to smack this child
It was your actions that gave her a scare
She felt threatened, and that the Oracle couldn't bare
So it defended her out of its duty and care
For I hear you were like a savage and wild

Back talk woman I will not tolerate
To me she and all should prostrate
I could have brought all back from the dead
Yet because of her, they all rot instead
Every single soul lost rests on her head

Now obedient wife, your orders are to dismiss
Or do you need to be told by my back hand's kiss
Get you and that child out of my view
Leave the girl cowering behind you
Or I will be force to . . .

Go ahead, let me be the one you strike
I will not let you harm on her a single hair
Where is my husband who once could care
I look in your eyes, but I do not see him there
More like Deadlock you sound and act like

With that remark, my hand rose
And in utter shock, I completely froze
Slowly I stumbled to back away
Rethinking of my sins from each previous day
Realizing the truth in all she did say

By the guardians, what have I become
Where did this monster creep out from
When did I become so sinister and vile
To threaten the wife that made me smile
To cast away a child in her time of trial

Oh Malon, what have I done
For how long did I have you shun
Though I tossed you to my side
Your love for me you still never hide
Always you were there, wiping away tears I cried

At that moment I began to weep
Yet behind her hand, every tear she'd keep
Soothing my shame with a touch so kind
Gently reaching down into my heart and mind
Bringing back her husband that had left her behind

There is the man I married
To whom I vowed to always be near
Rest my love, for we are here
Would you hold your daughter, my dear
By you she waits to be carried

Taking my child carefully in my arms
I was uplifted by her tender charm
The first moment I held her since she was born
Yet it was interrupted by a sound of a horn
For trouble was lurking, this it did warn

Lurching to the sorcerer making the desperate call
Gazing with my own eyes what lied over the wall
In the distance, orbs of silver and red gleam
Across the hills the dark fallen lords teem
Their leash being tugged by the very demon supreme

Get all civilians to the opposite gate
To the forest groves they must evacuate
Have all able wizards mount a defense
Use the guardians only as a fence
Do not emerge in any type of offense

Malon, take the children and follow the forest path
To the academy where you can escape Deadlock's wrath
I must stay and thwart this vicious harrier
If I fall, you will be the Phoenix's carrier
And you will be safe behind the royal barrier

Please my dear, do not make this your final perch
For it is alright to admit to defeat
If you get the chance, make your retreat
Then in the queen's chambers we can meet
Find me my love, never give up the search

As my wife with Talon and Mira quickly ran
I focused my attentions to the onslaught and clan
But to my surprise they arrived to a sudden halt
While not preparing any spells to rain their assault
Nor was a single guardian released from their vault

But Deadlock was waving his magician's spike
Then into the ground the staff vigorously did strike
The sound equal to what a thousand bolts deliver
Upsetting the earth into a ferocious quiver
And releasing a flow of a mound cracking river

Then a rapid slither caused the floor to rumble
Uprooting some while other's like me stumble
As around the town the burrows wind and coil
Scarring the dirt, making it singe and boil
Till the Lava Cobra's head protruded from the soil

And throughout the village, its body spoke
Slowly strangling all in a molten choke
While a volcanic venom it began to spew
Setting all in searing fire within its view
Leaving everything to dissolve in its acidic stew

And as I was about to summon the Phoenix by my cane
I was suddenly stricken with a paralyzing pain
Causing me to fall to my knees while clutching my lobe
For within my skull it felt as if something pulse and probe
And with each beat, a vision began to strobe

No . . . do not cause my mind to cloud
                    Out of ashes, into light
I will not let this be allowed
                    You will come to witness this sight
I beg you, do not show
                    Stumbling from the tallest height
I am needed, I must go
                    All you see, he shall smite
Nooooooooooo . . .

Now in a chamber with tortured souls
Where the flesh was burned instead of coals
The innocents squashed like fruit from the vine
As skins floated in a cauldron of their own wine
The latest feast for the heretics to dine

And over my wife's remains stands a man in hood
Stirring her blood with his staff of blackened wood
Glaring at me with Deadlock's drained complexion
Yet shimmering a view of my own reflection
The faces swapping in a rapid succession

As all insanity unlocked in his wailing cackles
The sounds clamping my limbs into shackles
While the ground crumbled leaving me on a ledge
The warlock then threw his staff as a killing edge
For between my lungs it now did pierce and wedge

And into the hollow ravine it had me lunged
Towards a wasteland of corpses I fatally plunged
Causing my limbs to desperately swing and lash
As I faced straight down at my inevitable crash
But before impact, I was swallowed in a flash

> Out of ashes, into light
> Rising in flames that will ignite
> To raise the fallen, to cure the blight
> Healing those who defend the right

> A young warrior forged from fire
> A child raised by the guardian's desire
> And the very creature whom all admire
> Will control the swing in moments dire

I pondered if this was the afterlife, was it the end
For I was in a land of pure light with no horizon's bend
As I walked, it felt as if I was suspended in the air
I called desperately for someone, but nobody was there
Only left with my voice's tunneling blare

Yet into a new land the lights started to fade
And I could hear songs of nature being played
Rustling of the fields and a wave's sandy hiss
The sky appeared in blue as clouds sailed in bliss
The ground became real, verified by each foot's kiss

And to my right side, into the waters the bluffs fall
While in the short distance pillars of earth stood tall
Appearing as fingers wearing rings of sea foam
The waves and currents they lightly comb
Making it look as if the mounds were able to roam

On the other side, pastures spread like a vast ocean
Winds send strange grasses into a swaying motion
Flowers with thorns while stems remain clean
Patches of ivy formed by tiny hearts of green
Such strange herbs I have never before seen

And a tranquil whistle in the gusts flew
But in it, a small off pitch quietly grew
The sound constantly nibbling at my ear
Till at last my name I started to hear
Becoming a shy voice that was calling me near

Turning with the direction of the algid breeze
I spotted a young lady overlooking the seas
Twirling around elegantly in a gracile hook
Greeting me only with a concerned look
Leaving me speechless as my nerves shook

Edmond . . . do you know who you see
Why do I make you feel so grim
Will I be pruned and be rejected trim
Do you wish for me nothing, just like him
Or do you accept and really love me

Gowned in ruby velvet with onyx lining
That aprons a Phoenix molten and shining
Arching over the fabric as smooth as skin
Its symbols also tempered in golden armlets thin
And dangling delicately beneath her ears and chin

Behind her neck and shoulders curtains her hair
Splashing on the arms the vest leaves bare
Spanning freely, the waves softly flow
Each thread a prism holding the sun's glow
As sunset clouds blush in her silk of snow

Within the emerald haloes where ambers comprise
A kinder spirit dazzles brightly in kitten eyes
Such beauty carefully engraved in her face
Her figure perfectly weaved and crafted with grace
So easily my wife's image she could replace

But then I was drawn to her shoulder's scar
On the right, shining dim like the furthest star
Staring at her, I realized it wasn't Malon I see
Wait, she was the youngling from the vision previously
And perhaps . . . no . . . could she really be

Yes . . . you are Talon of my blood
Yet you are supposed to be but a mere bud
How did you blossom into this flower
Have I awakened to a different hour
Did you revive me with the Phoenix's power

Answers for me you never had
Only questions that left me to grieve
Is that all from you I'll ever receive
Oh, there is still hope for us I believe
Please . . . do not be like him, dad

What is my connection to this person you fear
Was he the one who brought us here
Why on foreign mud do we stand
What has happened to our native land
"Just like him" . . . I do not understand

You know the answers to your why and how
Besides those are no longer your concerns
Except for the last which you speak of now
Focus, do you not see what she yearns

Behind me was a silhouette speaking the foreign tongue
With a familiar scar on the left shoulder burning like the sun
Then suddenly he was engulfed within the Phoenix's flame
Relieving my fears that he and Deadlock were the same
Yet causing new worries, for I know not his name

I understand the words and phrases you preach
But alas, I am unable to answer in that speech
Tell me, who are you, why do you have the Phoenix's bond
Does this mean I am with my family in the great beyond
What is happening; please, I beg for someone to respond

Do you prefer me to speak in your verse
Does it really matter in what words we teach
You already seek help in the far ends of the universe
While all the guidance you need has been near in reach
Trying to help prevent your fate from becoming worse

You are quickly reaching the end of the trail
Nothing can undo the destiny into which you are born
You already have witnessed that you will fail
But do not cease your fight, this I warn
For in certain circumstances you can prevail

Already your presence in this world will remain
Your blood survives through your daughter
She will be the one to cleanse all disdain
She will be your world's purifying water
And right now she tries to help wash your stain

But so many people my past actions alienate
To aid in my time of redemption is now too late
If all you say is determined and not a prediction
And if fate is left to control my future position
How can I then complete any acts of contrition

It is never to late to be forgiven
The path now you are still able to choose
Repent, and a new life will begin
Or if your pride you cannot loose
Then you'll be like him . . . lost . . . in . . . sin

Then instantly he morphed into Deadlock
And sending me into a frenzied shock
Then again in his blaze my flesh tore
As my anguish was released in a primitive roar
Yet finally I was released from the dream I'd snore

Somehow my death I once again evaded
Yet to call it luck, I couldn't be persuaded
As I uncovered myself from the blanket of rubble
While wiping off my face the charcoal stubble
I looked upon a scene that'd make any soul troubled

The entire town the Lava Cobra had succeeded to raze
For not even a carrion flickered in the remnant haze
Thus leaving nothing for the Phoenix to restore
Just a black desert that salted the floor
With barely any ruins capable to explore

Yet a carried sound made my ear lift
And towards the source I cautiously sift
As I neared though, the air no longer cried
But heavy panting then became my guide
And finally exposed someone trying to hide

There Mira was shivering with Talon in her grasp
Standing petrified with each breath having a nervous gasp
For she did not know if I was a welcoming sight
Still recalling what I almost did to her earlier tonight
And now she's left to defend herself, a child's worse fright

But this time I made sure not to rush
Just motioned to let her breath steadily hush
Then allowing her cheek to rest on my palm
Letting my own body's warmth be her balm
And giving the time she needed to be clam

All questions I had for her I willing spared
For the answers already her welling eyes shared
Then at last, into my embrace she spears
Able to be a child to freely shed her tears
While I be the one to soak up her pains and fears

How I wished I could do more to help her relax
Yet time was short, and I needed to give the painful facts
So as she finally had settled into a sniffling mope
I helped her prepare for the journey she must cope
For she and Talon were our world's last remaining hope

I'm sorry to place a burden on you so soon
But the heretics believe all are but a dune
You must find the academy where the royal mages stay
Call on your guardian, for it will help provide the way
While I remain here to keep Deadlock in disarray

I will fight till my right to the fire is extinguished
And then to Talon the Phoenix will be relinquished
So on your journey, it too will aid to protect
And when you arrive, many questions you can expect
Answer all you can, make sure no detail you neglect

But do not worry, for you will be safe there
Mention Malon and the queen will take you in her care
Tell her everything that she asks and needs to know
And the Oracle's visions be sure to show
Now hurry my dear, for you must go

Wait Edmond . . . I'm sorry I caused you so much strife
And that my guardian made your body and mind blister
You still helped save me, I owe you my life
And though I will never be like your wife
I promise I'll care for Talon as a big sister

No Mira, I thank you and the Oracle, for two lives you did save
A second chance for me and my daughter you both gave
In you, Malon's likeness I can truly see
And I know you will grow into a beautiful lady
I am honored to have a second daughter in my family

Now run my child, but do not be seen
Make sure you and Talon get to the queen
Take the grove's trail, use the forest as your cover
And as you both grow older, take care of each other
And please remind my daughter, that I will always love her

With a lonely smile spanning broad
Mira gave a single, reassuring nod
Struggling still to keep her eyes dry
Yet holding back with one giant sigh
As she whispered to me her final goodbye

Then wrapping herself and Talon in cape and cowl
Off they went following the night wind's howl
I watched as towards the forest they quickly wade
As in the distance their figures blended in the shade
Waiting until they enter the trees and completely fade

After watching Mira take Talon in her care
I started to walk right into the demon's lair
To stare death down eye to eye
Knowing this is the place that I will die
Yet still willing to defy fate in one last try

A lifeless volcano now the hill of his ants
Echoing the dark arts through gloomy chants
And my presence already known as I entered the caves
For I was surrounded by gleaming eyes and staves
Forced to deal with the heretics in relentless waves

The resistance I met was numerous and fierce
Yet through the defenses my guardian and I did pierce
As it set robes ablaze and used its claws to maul
While I casted spells making parts of the cavern fall
Attacking anything that was willing to brawl

All the time screaming for my rival by name
Purging forward while his minions we'd tame
For the warlocks cowered at the Phoenix's screech
Even mercy from me some soon dared to beseech
Till finally Deadlock's chambers they let me breach

There, the dark master ordered his army to the shelf
Saying that he would handle me by himself
Laughing at me with ranting words to intimidate
Yet I already had seen and accepted my fate
I was just stalling for time to make it arrive late

So you are the worm bestowed with the Phoenix's grace
You are such a fool to have even shown your face
Though it does save me the time in finding your trace
But I do really enjoy giving a mouse a good chase
And never has one dared to enter my place

Normally I like to use a witty tongue
But now that game is over and done
I did not show just to play
I am here to ensure you never get your way
In the name of all those you had to slay

Such a fine job you have done to protect
This the deaths of your family and friends reflect
Showing you are unfit to wield the powers you accept
To help the weak is but a foolish concept
For with great power, one demands great respect

Oh how I used to think the very same
But respect without honor is nothing but shame
Acquiring great power doesn't make you a winner
All it does is turn you into a sinner
In reality, you are no more than a sore beginner

For a sorcerer having the greatest of strengths
You turn to the most desperate of lengths
Letting your fears of defeat drive you wild
Having others ensure your rivals' corpses are piled
Even going as far as hurting an innocent child

Really, it is sad the path you choose
For you never had anything to lose
Others' triumphs you always seek
And your own you neglected to peak
In the end, that is what makes you weak

Insolent jester, who do you think you're talking to
Do you not know what I am capable to do
I will make a fine example out of you
So future brats can have a clue
Realize now the true power standing in your view

At that point, there was nothing left to say
So now I would let destiny have its way
Just responding with a silent, stern glance
Poised with confidence, prepared in stance
Giving a smirk saying "I'll take that chance"

My staff gladly initiated the first twirl
Unleashing at him anything I could hurl
Recalling all spells I learned in the past
From blizzard rain to a super nova blast
Each one thrown consecutively and fast

Through the tunnels my explosions did ring
Yet none were able to make Deadlock sting
For my bolts of light he could easily parry
Picking my orbs of fire like they were a cherry
Always adapting to my patterns that I tried to vary

While my Phoenix too he had stumped
For the power of two guardians he lumped
Leviathan now the new recruit on his team
And it collided with the Lava Cobra to make a poisonous steam
That left me hallucinating as if in an illness' dream

While in the thick, putrid clouds I coughed
Shadows of Deadlock laughed and scoffed
That on sight I'd swing my cane at as a spear
Yet in broken mist the image would disappear
And another would then lurk from the rear

Soon many more clones did circle and hound
Forcing me to desperately swing my staff around
Hoping that the true vulture I would find
For now my senses were completely blind
Only in luck was I now confined

Then suddenly, I started choking in a strangle
My legs started to numb and began to dangle
Out of my veins, blood began to pour
Drops rained a trail onto the molten floor
As I was pushed to an edge where the ground tore

All momentum stopped by his staff's impale
Now my life slowly started to exhale
Yet I am not ashes yet in an urn
The fire within me continued to burn
To scorch the monster, giving him pain in return

Enflaming myself with all the energy I could manage
I grilled the villain and was able to cause some damage
Bringing his face to shrivel and slowly melt
While his limbs started to bubble and welt
Yet Deadlock seemed to sustain the pain he felt

A small price to pay as my flesh does sear
But soon my boils shall disappear
The powers of your Phoenix draw to me near
And forever I'll churn my army of fear
To fill this world with darkness and drear

Soon my powers and life force began to dwindle
For even all I'd see started to wobble and spindle
Yet before finally yielding to my end
I was visited one last time by an old friend
Now the answers to the riddles he did send

Out of ashes, into light
Risen in flames that ignite
With a mix of blood, three souls unite
And together, one spirit takes flight

Lending to her its shine to cure
Able to cleanse the spirit and make it pure
With him, helping to cast away evils that lure
Infusing him with strength and courage to endure

She will be the one all come to admire
He will be the one who will inspire
The talon of the Phoenix's desire
And the warrior born of the guardian's fire

The Oracle visiting me even at death
Giving me one last vision while I still have breath
Finally his name is no longer a mystery
All his deeds and triumphs I clearly foresee
And a wonderful fate for my daughter he reveals to me

ha . . . ha
Ha . . . ha
Hahahahaha
HaHaHaHaHa
HAHAHAHAHA

So madness now your soul will consume
For your wife and child have met their doom
With them in chariots of death you will loom
For as you see, the fire now becomes a mere plume
With your family dead, the right of flames I will assume

Wrong foul heretic, my bloodline now still flows
My child still lives, and to her the Phoenix goes
And you cannot find her now, it's too late
For the Oracle has been showing me her fate
Along with yours, which I'll share to make you irate

Yes, today and for years you will be able to live
Yet confined in this hideous figure that I now give
And here will also be the very sight
Where you will cower and fall in a fight
To that mysterious man shrouded in the Phoenix's light

For you will be defeated by his hand
And he too you can't find, for he's from a different land
You will never have the Phoenix's fire
Not even now after I retire
You only start the way that will transpire

And to think, he is summoned from your minion's call
So because of your own evil, you shall fall
And I have you to thank for reuniting me with my wife
For finding the man that will protect my daughter's life
We'll watch her grow beautifully, while you decay in your own strife

Out of rage, he then casted me over the cliff to my death
Yet seeing me fall only brought more anger to his breath
For he would not gain control of the guardian he wants
And the caverns played my laughter that echoes taunts
As I screamed a name that in his mind today still haunts

KEEEEENNNNNNNNEEEEETTTTTHHHHHHH

Daughter's Lullaby

My child do not weep
Close your eyes and sleep
Press your lips on your thumb
Let all worries go numb

As the sun sets in the west
Lay your head down to rest
If a shadow should cause fear
Know that I will be near

Just hug your teddy bear
Whisper together a little prayer
Be snug in your fleece
Let your heart be at peace

Look to the stars in the air
For all your wishes shine there
Above the clouds and jet streams
You'll find the world of dreams

There a princess you can be
Visit pastures where ponies run free
Uncover treasures in the sand
Travel through your own candy land

Have a tea party with friends
Find where the rainbow ends
Hear tales from a friendly gnome
Make a flower your home

In a choir of snow you can sing
Let the autumn branches be your swing
Fly in summer skies of blue
For all seasons are chosen by you

After you've had enough fun
May you be welcomed in the sun
In the warm morning light arise
With twinkles in your pretty eyes

And I'll be there by your side
With my arms open wide
Giving a hug to greet you
And together start the day anew

How my thoughts swagger like those drunkards find
As light now appears as clear to the blind
While untamed seas drift behind the port block
And not even a peep is able to escape through a key lock

I thought I had found my one true muse
Yet again my heart suffers from foolish abuse
Her secrets I thought were only mine to hear
Yet I fear she whispers in another's ear

All I produce is scratches from a dried quill
While the other pen smooths a generous spill
The lives of my children now abandoned to shatter
While she births his offspring to pitter and patter

Oh how the world refuses to turn to me its back
Forcing me to witness what reality continues to lack
For my candle melts within the sun's frigid light
And all the mysteries lay in plain ole sight

Where is the voice that soothes my headache
The sight at my side that mends the day break
The touch that sets my soul ablaze in wild fire
The heart that copulates with my same desire

Oh but I do not yearn for just a mere visit
Nor something similar that complements an exhibit
I wait for the lyrics that will complete my song
The one harmonious note that I've been missing all along

For she will be the book with pages of white
That once opens will send my quill in flight
Her every turn breathes setting sail my pen's feather
As our story we will caress and write together

Born into this world like everyone else

Being the person the way God created me
Torn though from society by my differences

Seeing my surroundings in a way no one can

Asked questions from all experts and scholars

Believing their studies can help bring connections
Tasked with tests and random experiments

Perceiving some common ground on both sides

Retention has always been natural for me

Numbers I can see through images and figures
Attention this brings to the massive crowds

Slumbers still bring me quiet peace

Labeled by some as an extraordinary person

Controlling my problem while able to describe it
Disabled in the mind many also have claimed

Patrolling from my family tends to provide my aid

Handing me everything I need

Formal challenges they do not send
Understanding me really only they can

Normal living they help provide me

Coping with struggles has made me strong

Sharing this gift I do on my own will
Hoping it will bring us all closer together

Caring for each other indifferently one day

Riddle With An Answer

I would be very careful with what you assume
Sometimes it is safer just to question than presume
Already much time this can consume
And with it everyday tasks cannot resume

Something simple that makes projects halt
Yet keeps secrets safely locked in a vault
Bringing the most embarrassment in a fault
Computers try to delete it with ctrl + alt

Usually this is followed by another
From a list of these, one defaults to "Other"
To an innocent child, this can't be father or mother
Many have confused left to be its opposite's brother

The key that will unbalance a song
That clouds the mind to make days seem long
It's favorite instrument being the gamers' gong
A five letter word that many tend to pronounce wrong

Lost Soul

The ghost abandoned from the mother land
All that once had meaning now at a loss
Only destruction is now bound to each hand
While memories are forever chained to chaos

Forgotten as being a proud and loving family man
Remembered now as their blood slaughtering beast
Once the praised and trusted leader of his war clan
Now the spoils remain for him alone to feast

The cruel visions of his past crimes continue to haunt
Reliving all the deeds of the masters he served well
Yet the state he's now in acts as their eternal taunt
For they just watched as planned while he predictably fell

For decades he traversed the sands to find the means to repent
Working for new masters that promised him the peace he'd need
But again their favors and rewards to him were never sent
And even at death's encounter, he was still forced to bleed

Leaving his sins still calling for a chance to avenge
Starving him the pardon they never meant to fulfill
Their betrayal now feeds the monster's hunger for revenge
And he will let his blades cry with their blood's dripping spill

Those labeled enemies will feel his pain
Knowing all remorse he will graciously deprive
They will come to suffer under his new reign
And forever regret leaving his breath alive

Battles will rage across the globe once more
Every scenario to be dictated under his control
The man to forever remain the spirit of war
Until rest can be brought to his tortured lost soul

Eran dos hermanas gemelas
Que se levantaban fuertes y altas
Que cuidaban a sus niños pequeños
Mientras estos jugaban monopolio
Moviendo diferentes figuras
Como coches, trenes, y aviones
Pero había un grupo malo
Que odiaban a las gemelas
Y todos sus intereses
Y planearon destruirlas

No olvidaré ese día triste
Cuando el mundo se paró y rezó

Y ese día feo y triste
El mundo entero sufrió
Los malos atacaron a las gemelas
Con dos aves llenas de inocentes
La primera ave asesinó la mente
Y la otra mató el corazón
Los niños lloraron con miedo y dolor
Mientras las gemelas caían
Los niños heridos morían
El águila aterrorizada se despertó

No olvidaré ese día triste
Cuando el mundo se paró y rezó

Modern World

A higher advancement so they proclaim
The time of wealth and endless fame
Yet everything hides a second aim
The modern world, such a shame

All are moved by an inner flame
A dream, a purpose, or the right dame
Yet those could be but a false acclaim
The modern world, such a shame

Too many pieces needed to play the game
Trying to avoid the shortcuts that tricks frame
Organization pretends to make instructions tame
The modern world, such a shame

The goals are undefined, the rules are lame
Always pointing elsewhere to find the blame
While consequences are out to only maim
The modern world, such a shame

Refusing to remember from where they came
No one wants to live under their own name
All just looking to be exactly the same
The modern world, such a shame

So much potential still viable to claim
Before our age history is forced to rename
Yet in the end, it will be what the past became
The modern world, such a shame

Soldier

Born of the madness from combatants of yore
Nurtured by the skin raw from the gore
Baptized in the blood from the flesh we tore
Bred in the chaos from the fires of war

Both the protectors and exiles of humanity
For every warrior is willingly imbued with insanity
Civil laws are just words of profanity
And organized society appears as a vanity

Though we appear to walk with the sane
Our hysteria we learn to control and chain
For what sensible person enters the lands of bane
And feels no fear or remorse to have a sibling slain

Yet we are the force that lets the world revolve
We are the species that continue to evolve
Any obstacle met we eventually come to solve
And to all generations our genes will devolve

Our family tree will continue to branch and climb
The pages of history will tell of our tales sublime
In every age we will always be in our prime
And our existence will be felt throughout all of time

Democracy may have been born from Athens' wise
But the Spartan defenders allowed it to be realized
Through a handful of soldiers the world learn to comprise
And allowed the modern Western world to fully arise

Freedom, honor, courage, strength, and respect
These were the values that Spartans vowed to accept
When the call to its defense the council did reject
The bravest of men still answered their duty to protect

A noble king led the small, willing procession
Eternal praise and fame was not the intention
Only to save their people from the oncoming oppression
Yet their deeds would leave history an everlasting impression

Clogging Xerxes' mightiest armies at the Thermopylae crack
Holding off the Immortals with their trained, strategic attack
Falling when brother Ephialtes betrayed their hidden track
Yet the last stand would preserve Greece's final comeback

The price of freedom paid by the blood they shed
Saving the ideals from which our society did bred
So honor the final request of the heroes fallen dead
To remember Leonidas and the Spartan three hundred

My Sleeping Beauty

I will never forget this night
The stars shining so bright
The sea dancing to the moon light

Passing through the fragile tide
Standing by each other's side
As feelings within me build inside

The waves whisper across the land
While our path is molded in the sand
As I hold your hand

My sleeping beauty, will you awaken me
Let your kiss set me free
The girl of my dreams, so real it seems
Will you be here with me

How I wish I'd have this chance
To have you in my glance
Praying this world would be true
That I could be there with you

Witnessed by the mountain's peak
A serenade I gently speak
Bringing you a smile between each cheek

For you are always on my mind
The most beautiful and rarest find
An angel of your own kind

Oh how you make my heart pace
Just with the sight of your lovely face
A lady filled with grace

My sleeping beauty, will you awaken me
Let your kiss set me free
The girl of my dreams, so real it seems
Will you be here with me

How I wish I'd have this chance
To have you in my glance
Praying this world would be true
That I could be there with you

Embraced by your tender care
Comforted by the feel of your hair
As your kindness fills the air

My lady so pure and divine
With a touch so precious and fine
Oh how I wish you would be mine

And if I must leave your side
My passion for you can never hide
For within you my heart resides

My sleeping beauty has awakened me
Your gentle voice sets me free
Oh the girl of my dreams is now real it seems
Can this kiss really be

How I've always wished for this romance
And prayed that I had this chance
To have you in my view
And to be standing here with you
To say these words so true
That I love you

Worn Machine

This is Epsilon-Zero-104 here to report
To undertake the mission you want to abort

Nobody ever knew that we had enlisted
The government refuses to acknowledge our story
We were the patriots that never existed
A unit that could never obtain any glory

An Epsilon . . . this mission must be in distress
      Hmph . . . just another cog to add to the mess

In isolation we became their war machines
While in reality, we were a short term solution
Sent to act behind the unscripted scenes
To help clean their self-made pollution

    You go with what has been provided
      This is all you get, that has been decided

The given objectives were never meant for us to win
Always we were out gunned while short numbered
Doomed from the start, only a disgrace we could've been
For the odds were set to have us over encumbered

    That operation was in the headline news
      How much of the funds did they abuse

Only with scraps were we replenished
Thus the mission we failed to complete
The administration's image we had blemished
And thus we were branded as obsolete

Again depending on a past generation
　　All he'll do is lead us to annihilation

Malocchio always welcomed us through their eyes
Farewells were whispers that made the ears burn
For my unit they made no secret to despise
As we walked near, away the heads would turn

　　　　　Think he will be our captain's
　　　　　downfall

　　　　　Hmph . . . I just know he'll
　　　　　crumble the defensive wall

For our country, we were always willing to serve
So we were still called on to meet its needs
Yet the orders were spun, we were tossed a curve
For we were to complete the commander's dirty deeds

　　　　　Yes I know that all is at a lost
　　　　Send him anyway, it'll help reduce the cost

All funds and care began to grow stale
In every operation we were sent with a slit throat
The government secretly wanting us to fail
That way we could be another scapegoat

　　　　　What if he nothing but a spy
　　　　That or he just cowered away to cry

I witnessed the death of all my friends
Now I can only be with them inside my head
Our moment of peace my dreams can lend
Till I awaken to realize they are all still dead

Keep your eyes peeled in case he's a traitor
Oh, I'll shoot first with no questions for later

This is my life, this is my death
To always be the prey to hunt
I the only one concerned about my breath
That allies and enemies have both made blunt

You are already an embarrassing sight
Tell me "soldier", why do you still fight

I am the figure of their shame
To still be alive I continue to regret
For them to want me dead, I cannot blame
But I won't let them kill me yet

I am here to finish the mission
When am I done, that will be my decision

Refrain

Looping down a strip in memory lane
While thoughts tear away from my brain
Searching the particles it deeply contains
Looking to piece any hope that remains

Yet the numbness the body still contains
The frost continues to clot my veins
Crystal shards pierce the heart with pain
While blinding eyes in frozen rain

Slowly tumbling in an endless terrain
Where there is no distance left to gain
Just emptiness for all light to drain
Eroding the flesh into single grains

All the sensations still drift and wane
The conscience tick-tocks around what's sane
Grasping the sub-reality it hates to obtain
Leaving the stricken spirit to limper with a cane

A prolong search with nothing found
Taking a rest, pondering on the ground

Worn face with a broken frown
Losing hope and feeling down

No rhymes written, no words were sung
No feelings shared between the young

Wilted and withered in the night
A lonely weed under the moon light

But hearing a gentle whisper in the drift
Causing my attention to slowly shift

Eyes turning curiously to take a look
Silent and stunned as my hands shook

Someone not seen in the familiar crowd
A figure molded from heaven's cloud

A figurine pure as the first winter snows
Skin smoothly tinted with petals of rose

Fine yellow threads from the halo flow
As from the sun reflect a golden glow

With twins of sky topaz that softly glisten
Singing a melody that have my eyes listen

Lips coated as lollies smooth and pink
Said to be sweeter than the Ambrosia drink

A perky arc spans between each cheek
Diverting all memories null and bleak

The diamond stumbles on me from the sand
As I now gaze at the fairest maiden in the land

A rapid beat my heart began to pound
Locked emotions the angel had found

Yet out of reach seemed this sight
Picking myself up to start my flight

Yet taking my hand, letting our fingers interweave
The soft caring reach asking me not to leave

Welcoming my stay with an innocent grin
As on my chest she rest her little chin

Letting her gentle head sink into my shoulder
As I wrap my arms around to softly hold her

The evening sun setting as we start to slowly dance
Two young hearts blossom in friendship and romance

Within each other's arms a moment of bliss
And emotions expressed in one simple kiss

The world staying still, so it would seem
Just me and my girl from my dream

Feelings written with paper and pen
As I think about her once again

Thinking of my special friend far away
Promising to hold her in my arms one day

Mother

A vast desert heated by battle
Brings stampedes of foreign cattle
To try to clog the endless slaughter bath
And herd all towards a more peaceful path

Now located in a small, rundown place
A group of infantry make the town their base
A short stop for a day's rest
Until their commander sends them to their next test

All now gathered around an armored truck
Hoping to receive a delivery from lady luck
For the holiday season was drawing near
And all were looking for a little Christmas cheer

All the soldiers were being distributed letters
With brownies, pictures, and words to make them feel better
Yet for one nothing was sent his way
And alone he sat on steps of clay

A greenhorn humbled and young
Tending to himself and cleaning his gun
Well disciplined, always doing what he's told
Yet never fully welcomed, always left in the cold

Yet for him that was not rough
For already this year he suffered enough
But to no one, none of this he could share
And really there was no time to even care

So there he sat baking in the sandy light
Lost in thoughts he couldn't dream at night
Until he was interrupted by a creaking door
And by a little girl sweeping dust from the floor

A glimpse of a dancing wooden handle
As grains and dunes built by a worn sandal
He watched as the broom kicked the dirt into the street
Then turned and waited for their eyes to meet

Now lost in a rustic, innocent stare
Glancing as the wind blew her dark, caramel hair
Wrapped in cloth drenched in oasis blue
Draping a scarf as white as the clouds in view

Smooth throughout her soft, delicate crust
Pigmented by glosses of bronze rust
Appearing to be no older than fourteen
A child so precious and pure he had never seen

And he was frozen within his own smile
Something he had not shown for quite awhile
Until the girl started to bashfully wiggle
And give a shy, timid giggle

Feeling as if he was in the way
He motioned to her that he would leave his stay
Yet he was stopped by her small tender hand
And slowly he sat back down on the land

Kind sir, why are you in such a hurry
I am quite fond to have you for company
Relax a bit and do not worry
Your presence here won't interfere with me

Her words left the man in a surprise stun
For she spoke so well in his homely tongue
And around the door the broom she did hide
Then taking a seat right by his side

You are so quiet, why don't you speak
Maybe the words I choose you do not understand
Oh do you need a different dialect like Latin or Greek
Or possibly words spelled out by hand

Oh no I hear you well my darling so sweet
Just surprised to hear you speak in my perfect verse
And not read me as a sign to turn in reverse
Oh forgive my manners, it's such a pleasure for us to meet

I apologize, I did not mean to intrude
Nor to appear that I just stalk
Very rarely with anyone do I talk
Forgive me if I came off as rude

Oh mister, do not feel any shame
I know you must be tired from your patrol
So by your tags I see K. Denton is your name
Why do you happen to be the leader in control

Yes, Kurt Denton, though the first I go by
And only a private I am
A soldier taking orders from Uncle Sam
Following the directions from that guy

He pointed to an old man smoking cigars
His breast covered with medals and bars
Barking orders with a grizzly growl
Some words sounding offensive and fowl

Well if all privates are like you, then I'd be happy
For he seems so harsh and full of vice
I wish more people would be more like thee
For you seem so courteous and nice

Thank you little one, such an angel you are
Do not worry, it is just his commanding right
For it is difficult leading others into a fight
And to be away from home so far

Especially when yearly celebrations are to come soon
Many wish to be back in the states
To be with families and propose to soul mates
Yet right now all these are visions under the moon

The closest to home is but a piece of mail
For some it helps them cope
For others, it gives them a future of hope
That somehow in the end all will prevail

And where is your card from someone you love
Or any messages even from a friend
Or will it arrive by another dove
Surely your family has something to send

My mother died when I was very young
And recently my father had fallen to what kept him ill
All my support now comes from the G.I. bill
My family now consists of me, the only son

This may be hard to comprehend
But I was brought up only by military rules
Broken down and rebuilt by their ideological tools
And I never really made the chance to call anyone friend

Nor had you the chance to be with a significant other
Such isolation I know is so hard to bear
And to live without your very mother
I see why love and caring you struggle to share

Then suddenly his belly started to burn
Letting out a roar as emptiness it did churn
And his stomach she began to pat
No lard felt, just solid and flat

Oh child, do not look so sour
Just suffering from the journey overusing my feet
And this day there was not too much to eat
But I will be alright in a few hours

Oh Kurt, in your state I cannot continue to see
To be alone in all that you live
I know, now your mother I will be
For I have plenty of time and caring to give

Such a kind and wonderful dame
Please do not go to trouble for my pleasure
Your words alone bring joy I cannot measure
By the way child, what is your name

Oh Kurt, call me mother, mom, even mummy
Now stay put while I fix you a treat
It's not much, but it will fill your tummy
For all grown men must be sure to eat

Up she sprung into the kitchen
Leaving Kurt chuckling and his scalp itchin'
While hearing plates and cups clatter
He spoke up with a nervous chatter

My dear haven't you done enough work
You should have some fun and play
But then again, it's dangerous out here anyway
Oh where do your parents now lurk

Oh dear Kurt do not frown
For my parents are somewhere around
Most likely doing errands in the center of town
Sometimes not till next morning are they found

And no matter what is the current scene
I am always doing a house hold task
For the house needs to be clean
Just this my parents simply ask

Out on a tray she presented him a dish
With wine, flat bread, and some baked fish
The sweet aroma he could smell
Making his lips and taste buds water and swell

Once in his grasp firm and snug
From behind she wrapped him in a hug
Saying next to his ear a little thankful prayer
Then wondering why he just sat there

Dear Kurt, do you need something more
Or is there something you do not like on the plate
If you want, we can go to the store
Let me see if I have something else, just wait

Yet he placed his hand over hers clasped
And smiled while he tearfully gasped
Nuzzling his chin on her cheek
Breaking the silence, he softly speaks

I have not felt a hug like this in ten years
This feeling I have missed for so long
A sense of home, a place to belong
To have someone to care about so near

That's ten years to long for someone so sweet
I hope all lost time is made up in my hold
But now listen to mommy, you need to eat
Come on now, before your food gets cold

OK mother, I'll do as I am told
But only if you promise me this though
That you will keeping hugging me and not let go
Just keep me a little longer in your loving hold

With a smile, her embrace tightened around his neck
And gently on his cheek she gave a tender peck
Then resting her temple on his head
Making sure he was happily fed

His lips smacking with flavors of rye
Quenched by watered wine a little dry
Enjoying the texture of every gill
Leaving some leftovers after having his fill

Thank you my dear, all was very good
If you don't mind, I can wash these
Let me get up off my knees
And do something for you if you would

Oh dear Kurt, do not be silly
Just relax and leave this to your mother
Oh my, it is starting to become chilly
I will be back with a blanket for cover

She took the tray to the sink
Where water rushed and plates did clink
Then retrieving a blanket when she was done
And on the soldier's shoulder she had it hung

And as the horizon filled with the evening dawn
The little girl let out a tiring yawn
Yet holding the blanket firm in place
And looking at Kurt with a smile on her face

Now putting her scarf up as a veil
For the wind became frigid and frail
And Kurt led her to his side
Under his arm so from the cold she could hide

My little one, how now you tire
Why don't you get some rest and sleep
Come, you can make my arms your nightly keep
Together we can watch the day expire

Oh Kurt, it is my duty to tuck you in bed
And make you feel safe at night
To give you a kiss on your head
And keep all worries out of sight

But this family now consists of two
And there comes a time were we must help each other
So now it is time for you to rest, mother
Let your son take care of you

He placed his gun and helmet against the wall
And into his arms he let the child crawl
Letting her head lay upon his chest
While she cradled in his arms to rest

Blanketed under the clear starlit sky
Signing to her a Daughter's Lullaby
The child calm and at peace in his lap
Together mother and son gently nap

..
. . .
. . . .
. . . . .

Wake up you couch potater
What? You think you're the caped crusader
Am I your alarm clock and humble waiter
Come on, it time to go, you can sleep later

Woken by the drill sergeant's marching band
Kurt awoke to find only emptiness in his hand
And the house behind him now nothing but rubble
He was worried that the little girl was in trouble

Sergeant, we cannot go
Till I find the girl that lives here
Have you seen if she was near
She has to be alright, I need to know

Are you wounded son
Did you get smacked by your gun
There's no girl around, old or young
Nobody was here, you were the only one

But she lives here, I swear
She cleaned and cooked me a meal
I held her tight, her warmth I could feel
Did you not see us resting together there

I never saw her under the sun's beam
Nor did anyone else from the team
She probably just someone from a dream
So realistic to you it would seem

That house's been abandoned before this war
Everything's been neglected, every little chore
Now it just grounds for rats and bugs to explore
Just a pile of mud and wood rotting to the core

Sorry soldier, but we leave today
Yet maybe this will give you a sunshine's ray
For a package was sent your way
Here, apparently someone has something to say

In his hands he felt the envelope so real
Yet it had no postal markings, not even a seal
No return address had been signed
Only his name on the front did he find

And opening the package, he was left at a loss
For there he found a string with wooden beads and a cross
And a letter from the child he found so dear
With words that left him smiling with a tear

My loving son, you are not alone
For I am with you in spirit and heart
Know that my image to you only I have shown
And in my family you now have a special part

I know you traverse a difficult road
Yet you do so with faith and virtue
This to me you have already showed
Just know I have been there with you

Know this path has been made by a higher force
Yet from the same power you have been blessed
Just keep traveling along this chosen course
And in eternal paradise you will come to rest

And for you there is a special place
For you there is a perfect plan
For you are filled with my loving grace
My son grown into a man

Yet if you feel alone or things become scary
Just call on me, your loving and caring mother
Whisper my name, for it is Mary
And I will protect you with my Son, also your loving Brother

I never had a place to call home
In the dusty alley ways I would roam
Over walls and bins I had to leap
Just to find some food or a place to sleep

During the days I was always on the run
In some ways it was kind of fun
Finding an adventure was never hard
Just had to sneak into a different yard

Yet many times I felt so alone
And tired of eating scraps off a bone
Shivering in the nights dark and cold
Or from strangers receiving an unwelcome scold

So for a family I would always search
Asking nicely from the windows which I'd perch
Yet that made some people hotter
Causing them to chase me out with water

Till one night I found a place with a vast lawn
And there I made my keep with a big yawn
In the window still I curled up and dozed
Till the next morning by a boy I had arose

Yet this one would let me stay
He even came outside to me to play
And placing food and milk by his feet
Giving me goodies to enjoy and eat

And I learned two younger ones called him brother
And a couple older were his father and mother
Thinking she would get rid of me maybe
Yet she picked me up and called me her baby

So into the family I made my way in
The yard was the place to begin
Then one day I was given my own bed
And allowed to roam in the car's shed

Slowly making progress into the house
Now officially taking the job to catch a mouse
Oh I hunted birds, snakes, and even rabbits
I know they didn't want them, but it's a force of habit

Before I knew it, I could be in any room
Even in the master's chair I could groom
Feasting from cans with savory fish
Or an endless supply of crunchies in a dish

Yet to all of them I started to feel so attached
Especially when the back of my neck they scratched
So at night I made sure all rested their head
Also giving them some company in bed

Helping out when one was ill
Or notifying them of a kitchen spill
In the garden with mother we walked
And to the sisters I often talked

Everything was wonderful and great
Until another guest arrived late
Battering her eyes so cute
Trying to give this queen the boot

Yet she at times was disgusting in my sight
And we had several rounds to fight
Yet I have too much class
And so I gave her permission to pass

Oh sure we still have our struggles
And all the territory is in a constant juggle
Yet even though we push and shove
Deep down we also share some love

Yet only this the brother has seen
In front of the others we tend to act mean
But really we get along just fine
As long as she doesn't cross the line

I've been with them for awhile
The kids come to visit me from miles
Oh! A worn shoe lace towards me flings
The one sister says it time to play a game of string

To say no though I don't have the heart
So I give in and do my part
Because even though I am now old
They all still love me in their warm hold

Whether shaking the hands of the brother
Or resting in the lap of the mother
Just having their hands over my fur comb
Makes me thankful to have a family and a place called home

I do not know when another chance did begin
How I was so wallowing in endless sin
Not realizing every deed done was all in vain
Till I started drowning in what my hands did stain

My past now becoming an infectious wilt
All pride and honor now replaced with unsettling guilt
And left all alone with no one to turn
Just thoughts of an eternity left to burn

Yet for some reason I was spared by the cross
A father came to me when I was at a loss
Oh my confessions to him were nasty and rough
Yet his truthful words slapped me tough

Every hour I felt that I would break
As together we dissected every single mistake
Until I recalled the day I completely shattered and cracked
When I took a sworn oath and to everything I turned my back

Nervously quivering, feeling it was too late
For scattered in pieces laid my fate
Yet the good father said that it was not true
I just needed a little effort and whole lot of glue

After a minute I gave a reassuring nod
Maybe this hole I dug could be filled with sod
Perhaps the father could be right
And who was I not to back down from a fight

All my rages and sorrows I poured down the sink
Turning now to my own blood, not a store bought drink
Took seven grueling months before I was out of rehab
And then I transferred from a meth to a crime lab

There I turned in my mob given fame
Replacing it with a common unknown name
Oh I still decided to carry a piece
But this time, it was issued by the police

For I wasn't given the slammer, just under parole
The boys in blue saw how I regained some control
Crime rings they asked me to help them stop
So I took the job and became a cop

For who else could better patrol every alley and street
And know where former shadows hung out and meet
Now with new brothers who showed true respect
And really it felt great to serve and protect

One by one my past was put behind iron doors
Law and order in the city I helped slowly restore
While on duty, I aided in ransacking each hood
Further cleaning during off hours with services of good

On my first day off, I visited a house
There stayed my son and former spouse
Offering them the first check, telling them this time it clean
That it was for my past promises that they never had seen

All I begged for was for them accept my apology and to forgive
And I understood if they didn't want me to visit where they live
Yet my pretty angel still has that loving and kind heart
For she would give me a slow but second start

I was allowed to visit and be with my son
Once a week we'd go spend time and have fun
His mother and I again started to talk
Sometimes all three of us would take an evening walk

A couple of years have now gone by
And I am still the renewed, honest living guy
Greeted by others when on the blocks we pass
And regularly welcomed at every Sunday's mass

Investing smartly with the money I bring
Yet with my first bonus I went and bought a ring
For the day before when I picked my son up from school
I overheard him telling his friends that his parents were cool

And on a typical evening walk, or at least they supposed
There to my loving wife and son I again proposed
So what is the status with us this day
Well, let's just say our second child is on the way

Pondering

Struggling with shadows in the bitter cold
Facing the still night confused and alone
Again facing the turn of the game of old
Still searching for the rules set in stone

Wanting the trail to my successful place
Yearning to live a life of glory and fame
Yet uncertainty's mask wraps on the face
Trying to remember the pasts of shame

Still haunted from guilt and fault
While stumbling weary and lost
Trying to shut pain in a beating vault
Hoping for directions with no cost

The answers are supposed to be easy to find
With all the choices to give and define
Yet still lost in realities of the mind
No clear darkness, no brilliant shine

Pressing matters that force a choice
Every arrow leads to a different trail
And not able to listen to one voice
Roads to cloudy futures still so frail

Distracted by the light of a new day
Supposed to have a path visible to see
The decision is left in my hands to find the way
But I am still hoping it will be revealed to me

It can be helpful, or appear ruthless and vicious
It breaks the ice, or makes blood run cold
Creates a welcoming character, or someone suspicious
These personas masks consequently hold

For some, it's supposed to shroud the past
Yet it can call for times to avenge
It should be where all pain and anger last
But it can feed inner ambitions for revenge

There were things I never wanted anyone to know
Yet I come to you with all defenses down
For my true identity I am now willing to show
To you I will reveal what this costume gowns

Stare into the eyes that once knew how to tear
Listen to the voice that used to quiver in fear
Realize now every single fault
Peer freely into the unlocked vault

Some see this person as kindhearted and mild
Others as a freelance, aristocratic child
Someone who knows how to have some fun
Yet a traditional worker always getting the job done

A person who's moved beyond a tragic strife
Who's turned things around and lives a happy life
I know this is the person you wish I would be
But I'm sorry to say that it is not the true me

The public thinks this is my personality
Yet it is the figure that I want them to see
For I haven't lived like this since I was eight
And on that day, I vowed no one would suffer my fate

So the mask I wear is not an icon of pride
It is a symbol to instill the villains with fear
Telling the criminals there is no place to hide
While ensuring the innocent that justice is always near

And your company I do not mean to neglect
I do cherish when by my side you stand
Yet to the good people, I made a promise to protect
And that is something you have to understand

The person everyone wants just bandages the scar
What you see now is the persona that really bleeds
So if you see my second ego, the true form isn't far
It is just waiting quietly to respond to others' needs

I know this would be hard to concept
To have to live with day and night
If you were to walk away, I wouldn't object
You don't have to worry, I'll be alright

So there are the answers for which you ask
Accept now the face you do see
My identity lies within the mask
For this person is the real me

Once again it begins to snow
The temperature's dropping below
Waiting at the place for you to show
At the moment you told me to know
Yet I guess you had someplace warmer to go

One more time I am forgotten behind
To the oncoming blizzard I'll be confined
Left only to be navigated by the mind
For I reach out hoping a hand I will find
But I realize that I am now utterly blind

Drowning in a sea of crystal flake
While being anchored in layers of cake
All my heat the winds slowly take
Into a tunnel of whiteness I start to wake

Just nothing more than a patted clone
Now left for ice to gnaw at the bone
As my heart freezes into a hardened stone
While I am left to wander all alone

In the frigid grip of the winter's curse
With no clear direction for me to traverse
And every trail only making it worse

Still pursuing as my eyes freeze shut
As through the cracks, tiny icicles cut
The pain leaving to ask all this for what

Must you wait till I am numbing steel
To then realize there is nothing to feel

Will you decide to continue on
Only after you find I am gone

It's so cold

. . .

Every journey begins in the early spring
To a stone every mile moves toward
At that point numerous paths can bring
Yet once past the boulder, you only go forward

But in-between marks, some decide to forever wander
For they fear or refuse to face the next unknown
While others are forced to stand by and ponder
Since the next barrier cannot be moved alone

So I choose the way with you by my side
Together this course and more we can endure
Yet soon you prefer to become the guide
And have me following your every detour

Having the directions continue to juggle
The route always gives a new bend
Leaving pebbles and dirt for my feet to snuggle
As we deviate farther from the trail's end

Again the main path blocked on your behalf
And I standing behind patiently aging
As you remap the passages that make you laugh
While I wait for the scenery to start changing

But you just prepare for another loop
This I slowly and sadly start to realize
So at the first juncture's branch I regroup
To find a track appealing to more than the eyes

This current pass seems to forever splinter
So to follow it would be a mistake
For many more I wish to traverse before winter
And only uncertainty another pathway will break

So don't be surprised to turn and see me gone
Maybe then the true path will finally awaken
And if with me you now wish to move on
You will find me waiting on the road not taken

Thou have wandered in many ways
Now you have reached thy rock
Only a response can open the lock
Find the exit of my words in maze

Two rivers flow into the giant sea
The golden sun behind it sink
All creatures different together drink
Divided by clan of the sand and tree

Thou have spoken of a wedding feast
The people in signs of the kingdom of beasts
Different families on each side
United now with the bond of groom and bride

The three waters bond into one
The man, woman, and Holy Son

Mirror

I woke up in a dream today
I listen to what the mind has to say
Surrounded with a family of my own
Reminding me I am all alone
A loving hand I gently took hold
Just touching someone burning cold
Looked into the eyes of children that care
Only at the shadows on the wall I stare
All our finances covered from my job
Shows the work in the sweat I sob
I had everything I would ever need
I cannot afford to even bleed
Someone there always watched my back
I am left now just to shatter and crack
Reflected the light in which I starred
Holding memories in every broken shard
So much ambition many did adore
The image does not mean much anymore
So much promise did I bring
Now I just don't mean a thing

Today is the happiest time of the year
The anniversary celebrating your arrival here
For you are this day's greatest gift
Many lives you kindly touch and lift
I hope you receive grateful tidings from all you know
And that every moment today causes your smile to show
With the rejoicing songs for you we sing
That many pleasures for you they bring

May the day be filled with fun and laughter
With memories to share from here on and after
May there be sparkles shining in your eyes
That they open to find a wonderful surprise
May the stars continue to shine over thee
Fulfilling your every wish and hope truly
May you always be blessed in God's tender love
And showered with His glorious grace from above

I wish you a very special and joyous birthday
May it be beautiful like you in every way

Imagination believes it is entitled a right to a turn
Truth knows this something one can only earn
'morrow's wishes try to make it seem real
Surprises often have the secrets reveal

Taking the time to fully mature and evolve
Requiring stone to soften and dissolve
Understanding sleeps and awakens deep inside
Expectation the hunter causing this to hide

Legends residing in pages not on a shelf
Offerings demand sacrificing one's self
Visually impossible for the naked eye to see
Experienced only between the "you and me"

Tomorrow

How I always dread to live in today
Forced to choose the direction of my every way
No more time to prepare what to say
Looking for one more reason to have a delay

Yet this moment can no longer wait
Arriving at her house to pick up my date
How I wonder if we are led here by fate
This I hope to realize before it's too late

And together holding hands as we go
There are so many things I want her to know
How my love for her begins to show
Wishing to be with her for all tomorrow

Yet the day did not follow the set plan
Still I tried to be the best that I can
Though it felt as if from me she quickly ran
And I began to believe she deserved a better man

So at night I laid alone in my wake
Reliving yesterday's every single mistake
Slowly interrupted by the day's morning break
Another today in which my heart can ache

And I don't want to let her fingers go
Don't let me hear the words I need to know
Let me forget the cold feelings she did show
Just let me have back my tomorrow

Walking on the streets through the pouring rain
Trying to drown out all of my lonely pain
Until shelter I received from someone's cane
Looking only to find her standing with me again

Being wrapped in her arms as she draws me near
Soothed by the words being whispered in my ear
Her gentle voice telling me never to fear
Through all the days she will be with me here

And now no matter where I may go
She will be with me this I know
Her true love for me she's not afraid to show
For now she wants to be my tomorrow

And it is okay for you to just let go
All the answers you don't need to know
For they will all come to fully show
Just make your today your tomorrow

Oh Lord enthroned in the heavens afar
I pray You send me Your wishing star
This I beg while on my knees
For others' I request that You please
For so many lives are in a hurry
Yet for them I always tend to worry
For those who may not have the time to share
Let me be their voice to ask for Your care
So I ask if You can share Your light
And let it shine on them pure and bright
Continue to watch over mommy and daddy
Please help them at every opportunity
Lend a hand to each of my younger sisters
Aid in their studies, and help find the right misters
May You bless all within my family
No matter how far spread they may be
And please protect every single friend
May Your love and guidance to each You send
Especially the one that I hold so dear
That in Your love you keep her near
Send a ray to all those I happen to forget
Even to the ones whom I often neglect
Spread the remaining light to those needing it most
Even to the people who now are a ghost
May You lift all burdens from their chests
While in Your grace the souls peacefully rest
And in the world, bring an end to all war
Fill it with kindness so people won't suffer anymore
Help put an end to all selfish ambitions that run wild
And especially watch over every little child
Guide us all to respect each other
To love everyone as a sister and brother

So I ask my star to be split into parts
That it may spread to the many hearts
A new gift of life for all to claim
This I ask in Your most holy name
And You know my heart still has wishes to ask
But I understand You will provide me the proper task
Already You send me Your eternal love
And help lead my path from above
So this last request I give is not a must
But if there happens to be left a grain of stardust
Even one so small that the eye cannot see
If You wish, would You save it for me

As I watched her country drift in the sunset
Thoughts of Esmeralda still stayed in my mind
Yet the words of my fellow friend I did not forget
Asking where the rest of his story could one find

Much of his story I still do hold
Many questions I know still remain
Why you ask did I leave it untold
Well, I was afraid to have to relive that pain

My journey though set to last awhile
So come now, take a seat
Listen now to each lost trial
Let me make Bard's story more complete

To do that, we must first turn to others
We start with the empire, and three brothers

Baron, the oldest; driven by thirst for blood
Receiving much pleasure from those his ax slain
All living were fair prey for the slaughtering flood
For he felt no remorse, shame, or pain

Seth, the middle; an assassin of stealth
Killing only his targeted opposition
No desire for blood or wealth
Only concerned with completing the mission

Marth, the youngest; he was able to forgive
Unnecessary brutality he did not persist
Allowing all captives the chance to live
If the empire's laws they did not resist

All three to help carry the empire's pride
To enlist in the army conquering far and wide

In the military barracks, each chose their own role to follow
To the front lines Baron went and instilled fear
In the assassin's guild, Seth decided to make his soul hollow
While Marcus pursued the sciences of an engineer

And in their positions, each earned great fame
Baron's spoils and abilities equaled to that of thirty
Marcus constructed masterpieces like a puzzle game
While Seth accomplished hits that never appeared dirty

Soon their stories became legends that spread
Outdoing the myth's that sit on the shelf
Many claimed they were whispered among the dead
So renowned that the emperor summoned them himself

For in the armies, he now made them the head
Now the most powerful force the three led

Baron's hoard sent loose to raid and pillage
Myths say their blood spilling is what dyed the soil red
For they took over a kingdom like it was a mere village
Leaving all he saw weak maimed and dead

Seth's works and bids were usually left unmentioned
Some found the public, but many more were done
And if his loyalty or skills anyone dared or questioned
They'd be lucky to wake up missing only a tongue

Marth became the blueprints of the legion's tools
Even revolutionizing his own brand of catapults
Unchallenged at castle sieges, that art he rules
And a master of putting a stop to resistant revolts

And as all three progressed in their respective rank
Into the empire more countries fell and sank

And the puppeteer with the invisible hand
Conscious to all with a network of spies
Slowly dictating his will over the land
Nothing kept from his ears or eyes

The empire was under Golmeck's vicious rule
A brutish savage and hungry cannibal
Yet knowledge backed up his strength so cruel
For he was more tactical then the fabled Hannibal

Countless are the invasions and battles he fought
All the war conventions he retained in each scar
He held sacred every planned step and careful thought
His rule spread like a plague in lands both near and far

Harvesting the world with the Grim Reaper's sickle
Leaving the veins of the fallen with but a mere trickle

His legions forged with the Spartan's morale
Breeding thoroughbreds in even the lowest minions
The strongest potentials he'd always corral
At the age where one couldn't form logical opinions

Thus, his attention the three brothers appealed
To gain custody, he did slay their father to death
To the young and older, this was never revealed
Yet the act was secretly witnessed by Seth

So the middle one decided to make his enemies close
All an act to avenge his father's final vow
Waiting patiently to spill the blood of Golmeck in equal dose
Yet not knowing his enemy's past he lives now

For Golmeck used hate and pain to raise Seth with ruthless care
Like the emperor before, he was grooming the empire's next heir

Cross Winds

Seth and Marcus had known each other
For both were trained in the same lessons to kill
Many thought that each was a twin brother
For they were matched in every skill

Never losing a breath in their hustle
Their feet carried them silently and swift
They were able to bend both bone and muscle
But keen precision was their greatest gift

Marcus chose the instruments of wit
Over his back a bow and quiver hang
Yet Seth preferred throats to be slit
Making throwing daggers his venomous fang

And with every exercise, the two would together assist
Yet as they continued to progress, it became harder to coexist

Mind you that Seth introduced them to the clan
Yet Marcus seemed uneasy at their arrival
And slowly the inner circle broke into ying and yang
And the two at the end would become a bitter rival

Several innocents of high figures hid in an enclave in the wild
And their final test was to perform a stealthy slaughter
Seth was to target the king's wife and unborn child
Marcus to silence Jill, the general's youngest daughter

This to prove that they could kill with no remorse
To fail or to back down would label one a traitor
And all abandoners would be brought back by force
They would be hunted down sooner or later

But the final blows were halted by Marcus' hold
And left the two viciously scuffling in the winter cold

A dagger now in Marcus' clinch
An arrow tip Seth's hands disguise
Both go for the stab, yet stop at a pinch
Staring with frozen anger in their eyes

Both now having to choose to be with the living or dead
Either way, the fight would still be called a draw
Yet Seth offered a proposition instead
A temporary truce under word of law

That one travels east, the other journeys west
And both train forward alone till their paths cross
Then shall they determine who is the best
And who will have their first and final loss

At first Marcus had no reason to stop the blood spill
Then he thought deeply, and saw the face of Jill

The conflict there came to a temporary end
For the agreement was made by both
Though now they no longer called the other friend
They would still honor each other's oath

So with Willard and Jill, Marcus continued to travel
While Seth became a vagrant mercenary for hire
Once of the same mold, now from the shell they unravel
Growing in their own ways and how they desire

The last two wolves remaining from that pack
Still on separate paths treads their equal
Tensing the senses and sharpening their attack
Both preparing for their future sequel

And as far as I know, they have yet to again compete
Yet something tells me that soon, their winds will meet

First Love: The History Of The Rose

The rose . . . one of the greatest symbols of love
An image of grace and elegant fashion
The purest of hues being as white as a dove
And the boldest red deep with passion

Yet for many, its origins remain unknown
The legends struggle to glorify its detail
Even the true story from where it's grown
Has been omitted from its founding fairy tale

For too long its birth has been a mystery
But I am here to share the missing pages
About a forgotten prince in the story of Sleeping Beauty
And how the rose and its traditions were brought to the ages

Recall that on a princess infant, a witch placed a curse
That on the sixteenth year the girl would die from a spindle
The ill omen the good fairies could not fully reverse
Yet it would keep her to sleep while her age wouldn't dwindle

There she would peacefully lay in wait
Until her one true love would arise
For their first kiss would end her slumbering fate
And allow the princess to once again open her eyes

Still this outcome the kingdom wished to prevent
So a plan the three fairies had amassed
And with the king and queen's royal consent
They would hide the child till her sixteenth birthday passed

Into the woods the three did carry her
While blanketed under a moonless night
For the trees acted as a mystical barrier
That would halt the witch from entering the site

The evil woman heard that the plan had engaged
But she was unable to block the fairies' route
The thought of failure left her utterly enraged
As she demanded their location from every scout

For years their location the witch could not discover
But the lost pieces begin when the princess was ten
The fairies knew she would be safe under the enchanted cover
So they permitted her to wander outside near the den

For after all, she was still a playful child
And she always loved to sing and dance
She even befriended the animals in the wild
So she was always within a guardian's glance

Whether within her sights, or remaining hidden behind a hedge
Every woodland creature was devoted to keep her protected
For they made sure she stayed far away from the forest's edge
And to warn the girl and fairies if any trouble was detected

Though one day she was taking a random stroll
The directions her instincts blindly led
Every turn she made difficult for her critter patrol
For she was running fast and staying well ahead

But soon her pace she began to hesitantly yield
For the way in front bathed her in the sunlight's stream
She began to worry if she traveled to the edge's field
For the fairies warned her about such a bright gleam

But in the distance there were more trees to be found
So slowly she moved to see what the light wanted to show
It revealing a small glade which the forest did surround
And in its pastures a strange white flower seemed to grow

The princess was nervous to leave from the shade
But then her innocent curiosity began to chafe
For there were no signs to prevent her to wade
If needed, she'd jolt back into the trees where it's safe

With caution, she delicately began to tip toe
Studying each flower's unique and bursting design
For they covered the area like a blanket of snow
While a hint of the morning dew had them shine

The deft touch of every petal was as smooth as milk
Each draping in a symmetric and elegant fold
Some were as soft as the thinnest layer of silk
And woven tightly in buds waiting to be unscrolled

The emerald green stems were unblemished and mostly bare
Standing straight and firm though remaining easily brittle
Dressed with a set of frail leaves matching in a pair
That appeared as tongues of ivy, though their size was little

As she moved closer to examine the timid flower
She inhaled an aroma so potent and divine
Savoring a flavor that was so tender with power
That it would encumber even the spring's sweetest pine

In the flowers' waves she calmly did settle
Embracing their fragrance that flowed in the breeze
Letting her little body sink under each petal
While staring at the sky as if she peered through the trees

Soon she gently fluttered her arms as if she was able to swim
Letting her fingers bristle each stem as if it was a harp's string
Watching each bloom sway like a bell to a hymn
And enticing the little soprano to harmoniously sing

Her voice drifted through the forest for all to hear
Like a haunting angel with a chant soothing and pure
To the glade's outskirts, all the wildlife began to draw near
But there was also another figure that it began to allure

Still humming her tune while fixing a blossom in her hair
She was trying to decide which of the flowers to pluck
Making her selections with the utmost of care
Choosing only the ripest ones for her apron to tuck

She ended her merry harvest after retrieving a dozen
And using her blue garter, she bound them into a bouquet
But she paused all movements as the crickets started buzzin'
For they were alerting that something was coming her way

She was frozen in fright when seeing a shadow lurch
Manifesting in the form of a person, though still unclear
But its movements stumbled as if not knowing where to search
And she sensed it was just as nervous when towards her it did peer

Each stalling step moved it closer into the field's sun
Allowing the blank silhouette to be painted in the glare
Revealing to the princess a boy that was rather young
And both remained still while in each other's eyes they'd stare

There stood a youthful prince a bit taller in height
For he was two years older compared to her age
With his feet bare and his sleeves rolled up tight
A cabin boy is what his simple clothes did gauge

As the boy attempted to greet her with a quivering wave
The girl's posture relaxed as she sensed no ill intent
A little smile and fluttering fingers in response she gave
For she perceived him to be a shy and honest gent

Babbling as the right words his tongue tried to wriggle
He mentioned how he heard her lyrics and that they were pretty
His bashful chuckle complemented her teasing giggle
And he stood there naïve as her voice gave a thanks soft and bitty

As the princess became bolder, towards the boy she darted
Giving a quick poke to his chest, away she then did race
Taking the prince a moment to realize a game of tag started
A little dumbfounded, he still ensued with the playful chase

The forest rang with the children's laughter so humble
As within the blossoms they continued to run around
While into the petals they would mimic the other's tumble
Before across from one another they willingly fell to the ground

Both caught their breathes under a patchy, shady shroud
Watching the clumps of nimbus having the sun masked
Sitting in the flowers, the princess joked they were in a cloud
Yet what she was called the prince then curiously asked

Now the girl was wise not to reveal her real name
And her true identity no story really knows
Though she was willing to reveal the alias she'd claim
For the fairies had dubbed the child Briar Rose

But he was interrupted from revealing his name to her
For both were startled when her answer other voices did echo
Calling louder for the girl continuously while moving closer
Then in the glade, the three disguised fairies finally did show

The ladies huffed with relief though were still perturbed
For they searched for hours fearing she was in danger
But soon again they lost their breath and became disturbed
When their focus made them aware she was sitting by a stranger

The young princess tried to calm them saying not to worry
But she was pulled up by the hand having her bouquet drop
As one of them told her to remain quiet for they must scurry
All of the boy's advancements the other two made sure to stop

The four ladies made their way under the leaves
As one pulled out a wand which she began to swing
Around them, faint threads of glitter she started to weave
And in a bright flash, the young prince couldn't see a thing

With a few wincing blinks, the blindness his eyes shook
Only to find that the four ladies did magically disappear
While with bewilderment he did frantically look
To his surprise, there was not a single soul near

He recognized that all the animals were now mum
Even the flowers were still in the quieted yard
To him, it was as if the entire outskirts had gone numb
Not realizing that the fairies put the forest on high guard

For several minutes he just stood scratching his head
Trying to contemplate exactly what he had seen
While in the distant sky a pair of wings did spread
And his view was caught in a pair of eyes keen

It was one of the witch's spies in the form of a crow
And it relayed to its master the visions of the boy
Though she scoffed and told her minion to let him go
Thinking the idiot's stupidity just found a false decoy

The young prince walked to the princess' bouquet
And from it, the girl's little blue garter he did retrieve
He stared at it wondering if they would again meet someday
And with the item in hand, from the glade he took his leave

Back at the den, the girl piled on questions with each tear
Asking when she can go back to the glade to see her friend
With sadness, the fairies said to both she couldn't go near
And for her safety, her escapes they would temporarily suspend

The girl rushed to her room while crying it was unfair to be alone
While on her bed's soft pillow she let her sobs confide
The flower in her hair was the only memento for her to own
For she watched it in her palm as the months had it dried

Often to the glade the prince did return
Always in his hand he let the garter uncurl
A trend he kept while the months and years did burn
For he always had hope that he would again find his girl

The blossom she still retained, though on a shelf it did sleep
As the time grew, once in a while its presence she didn't neglect
Yet she was eventually permitted to again travel around the keep
And some say after five years, her true prince she finally met

The rest of the story continues towards the original tale's end
When her sixteenth birthday the kingdom prepared to celebrate
The young prince, now a grown man, was to attend
Though a visit to the glade would make him arrive late

Already the fairies and princess made the castle their home
But that decision unfortunately they made too quick
For hidden within the crowd the witch did roam
To make sure that on a spindle the princess' hand did prick

As some versions of the story have recorded to tell
Remaining in her finger was a shard and piece of thread
And the witch used this to enhance her evil spell
For so long as they pierced the girl, she'd be as good as dead

The witch believed the splinters none could find
For their tiny size would make them easy to miss
And to her spell the princess she will forever bind
As she would never awaken, not even to her first kiss

Along his travel, the prince caught news of the event
The beauty described resembled that of the girl he did see
The thought of harm coming to her made his heart lament
And he hurried to the castle in hopes of stopping this tragedy

At the gates, he found it was enchanted by the fairies' power
For in a deep sleep the entire kingdom they did encumber
Already the princess they had moved to the tallest tower
Where she rested gently in her forsaken slumber

Now the evil sorcerous had seen the young prince arrive
Still she feared the fairies' prophecy given when the girl was born
She summoned her wicked minions with orders that he not survive
And began engorging the castle in vines and branches with thorns

Every soldier moved in for a relentless attack
As the vines' razors coiled and tore at his skin
The prince did everything he could to fight back
But he had no weapons and wore only cloth that was thin

Though out of the vines' serpent strangles he broke
And he lost many ranks with each turn and detour
Yet the toll was starting to make his lungs choke
And a trail was left as his blood continued to pour

The witch's thorns spread like an infection viral
But still the prince was able to reach the tower's stairs
Slumping on the walls, he struggled up its spiral
Only to find at the top the evil woman standing there

A vicious joust from her staff brought the man to his knees
As she pulled the handle out, he fell forward and lied still
The witch watched without remorse as the prince did wheeze
And waited till his silence confirmed she made the kill

Yet there was no pleasure for her from his doom
For she found she could not open the tower's gate
The fairies' magic prevented her from entering the girl's room
And the fact that a man was this close just made her more irate

In anger, she ordered all her armies in the courtyard to disband
Then transforming into a dragon, she took to the sky
Flying over the enchanted woods that protected the land
Until a familiar glade she suddenly did eye

The one her dark memory clearly did discern
For it was the place the crow revealed that boy
Realizing the princess had been there made her rage burn
While the forest she couldn't harm, that field she'd destroy

At the petals her charred branches and thorns did tear
While violent cyclones had the emerald stems snapped
Her chaotic fumes distilled the once fragrant air
As the forest rumbled with her roar while away she flapped

But back at the tower, the unexpected did occur
As the hinges slowly creaked from the opening door
For below the ailing prince was still able to stir
And he crawled along desperately across the floor

He caught her draped wrist within his weakening sight
With one arm, towards her he continued to drag
Nearing her bed, he mustered the will to lift himself upright
While the pain and his own blood caused him to gag

All the energy left was focused into his stare
And it confirmed what he wanted to know
That he knew the beautiful lady sleeping there
For she was the same girl he met at the glade years ago

His legs were losing the strength to stand
As his vision of her began to split and blur
Suddenly he collapsed, falling by her hanging hand
Yet he was thankful that his eyes last image was of her

In one hand, her little garter he did tightly clutch
While the other reached for her fingers dangling at the side
Bringing them close for his kiss to gently touch
And calling her name . . . Rose . . . one last time before he died

Yet luck or destiny had guided him to her finger tips
For the one he selected contained the needle point and flax
And both venomous fangs were drawn out by his puckered lips
Thus with his final act, the witch's spell he did relax

But as it is too often, fate's kindness was just as cruel
With his kiss, the evil enchantment would not be reversed
For only by the one true soul mate the fairies' gift did rule
And sadly this was not her chosen love, he was just the first

From the violence of the battle, the three remained hidden
Though they did appear to cleanse the mess
They recognized the prince as the boy once forbidden
And his last actions they mercifully did witness

They even felt a dark spell lifted from a tiny spot
For in his lips they removed the pieces the spindle did stick
They even saw on the princess' finger a small clot
And determined the prince had removed the witch's secret trick

Their hearts were filled with grief at his death
Regretting that from him the princess they did hide
How they wished they could restore his breath
Even more so when they found on what he lied

Clinging to his belt were twelve flowers together strung
Which they knew from the glade's field he did lift
The same number and bundle when the princess was young
And this batch was meant to be her birthday gift

Seeing this, the fairies knew how to honor all his deeds
For in these blossoms his memories would forever flow
From his bouquet, they collected all the seeds
And within the witch's branches, each one they did sow

Then with their magic, the skies cried for his pain
Refreshing the lands within cool crystal water
Nurturing the dried stalks that pleaded for rain
And shrinking the vines that were meant to slaughter

The once deadly plants were each made into a bush
Their stems now a familiar green though kept their thorns
From the tips, small shoots they began to push
For the glade flowers were starting to be reborn

From the shrubs that had only water to consume
They sprouted the white petals radiant and pure
But other stalks had different colors to bloom
To help remind what the prince had to endure

For some roots were quenched by the blood he shed
Others had it mixed with water to drink
While some flowers blossom in a rich deep red
Others had crimson blots or were fully in a soft pink

In the glade, the rain replenished its tranquil dew
And the white flowers again grew within its care
Though now along with petals of a yellow or orange hue
To remind that the children's friendship grew in the solar flare

All this was completed before the setting sun
And back at the tower the fairies did reconnect
For there was still one lingering task to be done
How to show the prince's remains the proper respect

They did not believe it should rot in place to the bone
Nor should they preserve his state that the witch did deform
And they refused to bury him alone under a cold stone
So it was decided that his body they would have to reform

Using their wands, he was turned into the precious flower
One that as long as the princess lived would not whither
This way he could be with her during every sleeping hour
For they felt it was right that by the princess' side he'd hither

The petals were dyed from his heart's passion and charm
The jeweled green stem remained smooth having one minor groove
For the stalk's soothing touch would do her no harm
And the furrow would remember how the thorn he did remove

How they wished his title the new bloom could acclaim
Yet they knew that another he would want to propose
For he would prefer that it honor the lady's name
So based on his last word, they called the flower the rose

Below her bosom the fairies had her hands fold
Letting each delicate finger gently interweave
As they gently blanketed him under her palms' hold
While on the bed, her little garter they did leave

While the princess slept, from all harm his soul did protect
Some say it was for a century while others for under a year
But it is known that her true love he did help direct
For his spirit was the guide that brought her prince near

It is said that in his breath he had the garter lift
And into her love's sight the winds had it flew
Her true prince would follow its every shift
Until the enchanted castle finally came into view

There her prince handed the witch her final defeat
And again he trailed the garter up the tower's well
Bringing him to her side while it rested at the rose's feet
And with one kiss, her true love finally broke the spell

Soon all the people were awakened across the land
And the princess was reunited with her father and mother
They were overjoyed to see their daughter with prince in hand
And were fascinated by the rose she held in the other

It was then the three fairies once again reappeared
And they shared with the kingdom the first prince's story
How away from the witch's plan he help steered
And that the rose was a symbol to honor his glory

The princess then recalled how she met her friend
And she was saddened with how he had to depart
But she was grateful that he was loyal to the end
And she would always keep him close within her heart

It is said that she always carried her rose with great care
Often wearing it on the vesture upon her chest
Or letting it be gently placed within her hair
It is even believed she still held it as she was laid to rest

But she declared that the rose should not symbolize sadness
Rather it should be a token that only brings one cheer
That it should celebrate others only with the greatest gladness
Whether they be a good friend or a loved one dear

True to her word, the roses were used for her marriage
For the white blooms were adorned to her veil and dress
While the other colors decorated the couple's carriage
Even throughout the church the flowers did bless

At the banquet, the princess' roses were the talk of each dame
So into the crowd of maids the bride playfully tossed her bouquet
While the little blue garter the prince still had in his claim
And towards the young bachelors the groom tossed it their way

Yet it did seem the recipients received a bit of luck
For soon to their true loves their gifts had led
And from then on, it became a tradition that stuck
Since for generations, the fortunate catchers were next to wed

Over time each rose was assigned a different love
Some were for soul mates, others for just a friend
Certain ones were offed to those in heaven above
While others only a thoughtful gesture they'd send

While its legends and uses will always continue to grow
The expression you give it shouldn't cause any concern
But if its meaning you still wish to know
Then this is the message it wants you to learn

Your first love you should never forget
To others your heart should never close
And your true loved ones you should never neglect
For these are the lessons and the origins of the rose

. . . *Good Morning* . . .

Sneak Preview

My servant, you may approach the court
Tell us what matters you have to report

Master, the Fallen's presence continues to be on the rise
But we have successfully concealed the apostles from their eyes
They are still deciphering what the manuscripts disguise
And we have them under constant surveillance with our network spies

Time is running thin for our spies to hold their ground
Have the candidates for the archangels been found

We have identified each potential subject's position
All innocent crime victims in stable or critical condition
The augmentations are also available for immediate transition
All that is remaining to proceed is your final decision

The time is now to call on those who will protect
Show me the top prospects the court wishes to select

What if you were offered another chance
To bring a pulse back into hands dead in time
If you were to awaken in flesh and blood newly enhanced
What angel would arise from the ashes of that crime

Subject D121, the only remaining survivor able to stand and bleed
His whole family slaughtered in the Heretics' riots with speed
Though a counter attack he was able to manage and lead
Records also show him with a strong determination to succeed

He shall take on Michael's role
For the chaos and others he might be able to control

Subject T317, his friends murdered in the crossfire of a Heretic raid
He tried to provide them comfort where they bled and laid
Even while injured, he pursued to give other victim's aid
A timid character, confrontations he prefers to evade

He shall become our Raphael
For he will fulfill the responsibilities well

Would you let your anger seek out its hungering revenge
Or would your compassion allow you to be any innocent's guard
Would your grief guide you to have any victim avenged
Or would your pain try to forget that you were scarred

Subject D815, widowed after his child's life had begun
Now he has lost his only son
Both victims of a Heretic hit and run
His thoughts are isolated, outside contacts he tries to shun

His voice we cannot permit to remain silent
He shall therefore take on Gabriel's assignment

Subject S3211, the latest victim we were able to discover
In a recent Fallen attack, they killed his lover
He would strike anyone who near her body dared hover
He tends to have outbursts which currently have him slow to recover

He shall be Azrael, for our enemies will not suspect him
A desperate measure as the time grows more grim

Would you ensure that our last drops of blood finally spill
Or would you direct how it courses in our next stage of evolution
Would you bring the entire world to stand still
Or spin it into a never ending revolution

Master, are you sure these are the ones to be sworn
For these men, already many scars are worn
Are you sure they will be able to handle future scorn
Are these to be the angels that have the new age born

They are the only ones who can meet every impossible demand
And their scars will make them able to fully understand

And when you find out that all was not lost
What would have been the final cost

Alright master Prophet
The enhancements these men will then get
I will make sure personally all precautions are met
And will notify you when the preparations for the next phase are set

Well done, let the recruitment begin
And pray that they will redeem our every sin

The Archangels are coming

Adam's apple—the forward lump on the front of the throat due to the larynx cartilage. It is usually easier seen in men than women.

badger—to annoy.

barracks—a military building used to house soldiers.

bloke—Australian and New Zealand slang for man.

blot—a blemish, spot, or mark.

bosom—the breast of a person.

cackles—loud laughter, usually portrayed as having a mean or unpleasant intent.

carrion—a rotting dead body.

cedar—brown in color with a reddish hue.

celestial—being related to heaven or the sky.

chafe—to irritate or annoy.

clad—having or wearing an outer covering.

clobber—to violently strike repeatedly.

clot—a mass that is semisolid, like blood drying at a wound.

coma más comida—Spanish for ordering in the second tense to "eat more food".

cumbersome—difficult to handle or navigate.

deft—nimble or moving with easy.

Don—mafia slang for the mafia boss.

dormant—not active or in a resting state.

encumber—to block or impede; weigh down.

Ephialtes—referring to Ephialtes of Trachis, the Greek man who betrayed his allies defensive position by showing the Persian army the hidden path at the Battle of Thermopylae.

erosionless—unable to be worn away.

flax—fiber from the Linum plant that is used to make thread for woven materials.

follicle—the skin organ that grows hair.

furrow—a narrow groove or depression on a surface.

garter—a band worn around the leg to hold up a stocking or around the arm to hold up a sleeve.

G.I.—term used to describe a member of the United States Army, initially referring to returning World War II veterans. Originally short for "galvanized iron", it today stands for "government issued".

G.I. bill—the informal term referring to the Serviceman's Readjustment Act of 1944 which provided benefits to returning World War II veterans. Benefits included low mortgage rates, loans to start businesses, tuition for education, and unemployment compensation. The term is still used today to refer to programs benefitting military members.

glade—an opening in the forest.

gracile—graceful and slender.

Grim Reaper—the personification of death. He is usually portrayed as an old man or skeleton wearing a black robe. He tends to carry a scythe or sickle as a reference to harvest the dead.

gruel—a thin or watery porridge.

Immortals—the elite force for the Persian Empire consisting of 10,000 men. It was custom to quickly replace any soldier killed or wounded to maintain this constant number. The Immortals were called on Xerxes during the Battle of Thermopylae.

incantation—a ritual of words or sounds used to cast magical spells.

jackin'—slang for stealing a car.

jaunting—taking a trip for pleasure.

jester—a clown that usually entertained royalty or noble people.

jobber—a term for a person or performer whose role is to always lose.

Leonidas—The Spartan king who commanded the three hundred Spartans and Greek alliance against Xerxes and the Persian army at the Battle of Thermopylae.

Leviathan—a word that usually depicts a large sea creature, monster or whale. It has many depictions in literature and religion.

lurching—to walk slow and unsteadily

made man—mafia slang for a person who has been fully inducted as a member into the mafia

magus—an ancient magician or sorcerer.

maid—a young unmarried woman.

maimed—to have a body part wounded or crippled.

Malocchio—a superstition in Italy for the all-seeing evil eye (mal meaning bad and occhio meaning eye). It is believed to be the cause of bad or envious thoughts that could affect the person they are depicted towards.

manifesting—appearing or revealing.

maul—to beat or badly handle.

mob—slang term for the mafia.

Mustang—a popular muscle car created by Ford in 1964 with updated versions still manufactured to this day.

necromancy—the belief in evil and dark spells, usually to raise the dead or cause supernatural effects.

Nile—referring the Egyptian river which is known for its flooding cycles and regarded as the longest river in the world.

nimbus—cloud.

nocturnal—related or occurring at night.

obituaries—the section in a newspaper or magazine that lists recent people who have passed away in the local area.

Phoenix—the legendary firebird who can be reborn from its own ashes and is a common figure across many mythologies.

piece—slang term for a gun.

P.S.—short for Post Script, usually something written after the main body and signing of a letter.

puppeteer—a person who controls puppets.

Oracle—a person or figure able to see and predict the future.

rabid—intensely enthusiastic or wild.

raze—to tear down and leave leveled to the ground.

savant—referencing savantism or savant syndrome which is a rare condition with a person having a brain injury or development complications while displaying profound abilities that are considered greater than normal. Such abilities can include having photographic memory, music skills, and excelling in mathematics. Though people with this condition tend to have a narrow focus and have hardships in socializing and concentrating on many items at once.

scoff—to mock at.

scuffle—to struggle or fight in close quarters.

sickle—a tool used to cut down grass or to harvest crops. It has a long curved blade on a handle.

snow blind—to be blinded or lose vision due to a bright flash or reflection, usually specific to light reflected off snow or ice.

soot—black residue or ash, typically from burning fuel or materials like coal.

soprano—a female singer, usually with the highest pitch range.

Sphinx—a mythical creature usually having the body of a lion and the face of a human. In Greek mythology, the sphinx had a face of a woman and was malicious to people who could not answer her riddles. In Egypt, the sphinx is associated with a man's face and is a kind figure often protecting an entrance.

spindle—the rod on a spinning wheel where thread is wound.

stash—slang for a collection of money or valuable items.

stature—a high level of respect usually gained from a notable achievement.

sublime—inspiring or worthy of adoration

Tassy—Australian term for the island of Tasmania.

teem—to move in large numbers.

Thermopylae—meaning "the hot gates", it is a place in Greece where the infamous battle where Leonidas and the Greek forces had their last stand against Xerxes and the Persian army at a narrow pass by the coastline.

tremoring—shaking or trembling.

tu familia en la finca—Spanish for "your family on the farm".

turf—slang for declared territory, commonly used by gangs or mafia members.

vigor—a strong force.

wade—to walk, usually in shallow water.

wallowing—devote or indulge excessively into something.

whack—mafia slang meaning to kill or to assassinate.

wriggle—to twist or squirm.

Xerxes—known as Xerxes the Great, he was the Persian king who invaded Greece and faced Leonidas and the Greek forces in the famous Battle of Thermopylae.

AVAILABLE NOW

Enjoy Michael Angelo Sippo's first poetry collection *Drifting Seasons* available now at AuthorHouse.com and other online retailers. Also available for E-Book!

Michael Angelo Sippo graduated from St. Louis University with a Bachelor of Arts in Computer Science and has recently completed his Master's Degree in Computer Science at Washington University. Currently residing in St. Louis, Michael works as a computer programmer for AT&T and is a member of the Almas Del Ritmo Dance Company. He performs with the dance team Salsa Sabor and is an assistance dance instructor. Michael is also a knight of the Belegarth Medieval Combat Society realm of Arnor, which fights out at Forest Park every Saturday. During his free time, he enjoys participating in the Salsa dancing scene and spending time with his family and friends.